Wanderings

Ken Weber

Wanderings

The publisher wishes to thank Henry Holt and
Company, Inc., New York, for permission to
use the quotation from *The Outermost
House*. That company requires the following
form of credit: From THE OUTERMOST HOUSE by
Henry Beston. Copyright 1928, 1949, © 1956
by Henry Beston. Copyright © 1977 by
Elizabeth C. Beston.

ISBN: 0-934881-11-1

Library of Congress Catalog Card Number: 89-81053

First edition: October, 1989

Printed in The United States of America

The Dutch Island Press
99 Brown Street
Wickford, Rhode Island
02852

For Bettie, forever

W hatever attitude to human existence you
fashion for yourself, know that it is valid only if
it be the shadow of an attitude to Nature. A
human life, so often likened to a spectacle upon
a stage, is more justly a ritual. The ancient values
of dignity, beauty, and poetry which sustain it are
of Nature's inspiration; they are born of the
mystery and beauty of the world. Do no
dishonour to the earth lest you dishonour the
spirit of man. Hold your hands out over the earth
as over a flame. To all who love her, who open to
her the doors of their veins, she gives of her
strength, sustaining them with her own
measureless tremor of dark life. Touch the earth,
love the earth, honour the earth, her plains, her
valleys, her hills, and her seas; rest your spirit in
her solitary places. For the gifts of life are the
earth's and they are given to all . . .

—Henry Beston
The Outermost House

Foreword

Before somebody beats me to it, let me say that the events and observations chronicled in this book are simple things. They will avert no national crisis, solve no social problems. They aren't meant to.

These ninety-six columns merely convey one man's perspective. Since I'm that man, they are my thoughts on what I find intriguing and perplexing, amazing and amusing, and quietly provocative, during my wanderings around the backyard and countryside.

The pieces, written over several years, are arranged to cover a full year—beginning with April, simply because I've come to consider April 1 my personal New Year's Day. Spring to spring. Full circle.

Each of these columns appeared in the Sunday Magazine of the *Providence Journal*. They are reprinted with only a minimum of changes. Local place names were omitted here and there, and occasionally a phrase was altered slightly, either to eliminate an unnecessary date or to regain a consistency of style. Otherwise, the columns are as they originally appeared.

I want to thank the *Providence Journal* and its Sunday Magazine editors, particularly Hilary Horton and Doug Cumming, for the freedom to write what I wanted and in the manner I preferred. Another big thank you goes to Johanna Hoffman, whose illustrations make this as much her book as mine.

Ken Weber

Wanderings

Spring

1	Sunrise service	3
2	Where spring comes first	6
3	Call of the dove	9
4	A precious secret	12
5	The dependable migrants	14
6	Fish are an excuse	17
7	Profane and profound	21
8	Plowing	24
9	May	27
10	Welcome back	30
11	Reaping the memories	33
12	Awaiting the orioles	36
13	The harvest of blossoms	39
14	The last dinosaurs	41
15	Whippoorwill	45
16	The art of sauntering	48
17	Foreverness of June	51
18	Rainbow magic	54
19	Teacher, teach-er	57
20	Thunderstorms	61
21	Friendly enemies	64
22	Morning on the mountain	67
23	Raspberries	71
24	The fiddlers	74

Wanderings

Summer

25	Haying	79
26	The performer	82
27	Summer in the orchard	85
28	Reward of the hummingbird	89
29	Water lilies	92
30	If I could order the weather	95
31	Cry of the loon	98
32	We almost didn't go	101
33	The swimming hole	105
34	A liberated sandpiper	109
35	Summer twilight	112
36	The initial tree	115
37	Catfish	118
38	The scythe	121
39	The insect orchestra	124
40	The fogs of dawn	127
41	September	130
42	Mount Oops	133
43	Warbler confusion	136
44	Fire in the treetops	140
45	Finally, our own apples	143
46	First frost	146
47	Chipmunk days	149
48	The numbers	152

Wanderings

Autumn

49	The hearth	157
50	Tipsy robins	160
51	Lure of the night	163
52	My own migration flight	166
53	Hornets and mixed feelings	169
54	October osprey	173
55	Return of the chestnut	176
56	Indian summer	179
57	The season of November	182
58	Woods work	185
59	Legacies in stone	188
60	A reminder and a promise	191
61	Wind and waves	194
62	Rusty	197
63	Giving thanks	201
64	Fury of the shrew	204
65	Snow fascination	207
66	December sunsets	209
67	Ice needles	212
68	The sycamore	215
69	Furry torpedoes	218
70	How do they know?	221
71	One tough bird	225
72	The winter solstice	228

Wanderings

Winter

73	Frozen to a pump handle	233
74	Fox on the hill	237
75	Last days of the monarchs	240
76	A possum in the yard	244
77	Invisible visitors	247
78	Old barns	250
79	Mouse tunnels	253
80	Seeing the wind	256
81	Bettie vs. the squirrels	259
82	Ice in the marsh	262
83	The beach in winter	265
84	Close to the stars	268
85	Half-past February	271
86	Beaver ponds	274
87	Skunk cabbage	277
88	The bluebirds of winter	280
89	March	283
90	Old grouch	286
91	Tumbledown brook	289
92	Deermouse tenants	292
93	Waking the toads	296
94	Promise of the buds	300
95	Dad	303
96	Resurrection	306

Spring

1

Sunrise Service

It's Easter, so I'm climbing a hill to see the sun come up. I'm not sure what I expect to find, but with today being Easter, this feels special, sort of my own sunrise service. I don't even take my dog along.

Just as midnight is significant at Christmas, so is sunrise on Easter. I want to see it from the top of a hill, surrounded by trees and ledges and boulders. It's possible to find serenity and inspiration, maybe even reverence, in wild places.

The forecast is for a clear dawn—although a frosty one—so I set the alarm for 4:20, about an hour before the listed sunrise.

Already, there is enough light to see quite well. I drive the mile to the hill and park beside a stream. I can hear a few crows off in the distance as I start walking up an abandoned woods road. Song sparrows are singing and I hear a blue jay or two, but there are few other sounds. A hush of anticipation seems to settle over the hillside. It's a good feeling.

On the climb, I think about perhaps meeting a homebound fox returning from its night hunt, but mostly my mind wanders over a dozen other thoughts; our family plans for the day, the past—and future—of this hill, my Little League baseball team, and even that first Easter.

I see no fox, but I tread as lightly as possible through the woods, trying to avoid stepping on branches and twigs. Noise would disrupt the tranquility, like coughing in church.

The eastern horizon, seen through the trees, is starting to glow both pink and gold. I have to hurry. The sun will be up soon, and I want to be on a certain ridge, where there is a clearing that offers a panoramic view of the eastern slope, when that happens. I want to see the very first rays of the day.

As I cross a small meadow, I notice the puddles are filmed with ice. In moments, I'm walking on the ridge. Halfway across, I stop. The sun is there, rising almost as if right out of the ground, a red-orange ball, not bright enough to hurt my eyes. For a moment, I watch it and wonder if those who came to the tomb that long-ago morning actually arrived at just this moment, or is that only part of a legend that has taken form over hundreds of years of retelling?

It's too cold to stand here, though, so I walk some more and swing around a little pond tucked into a hollow. I'm in shadow again because I've dropped below the ridge, so I pull up my hood, wait a few minutes, and watch another sunrise. Now, the sun is fiery yellow, and it hurts to look directly at it. It tinges the edges of some clouds, painting them in exquisite gold.

Still no foxes, but more birds are singing and the wind is rattling some leaves and branches. I take a trail down to a paved road, cross it, and walk on down toward the stream. By now, somewhere, church services are in full swing with bundled-up congregations singing the old hymns and rejoicing over the Resurrection. Suddenly, a thought pops into my head: I wonder how many women are wearing Easter bonnets. They're corny, I suppose, and Bettie won't wear them, but I still like seeing them on Easter morning.

Once more, I'm in deep shadow as I continue descending the hill. Already, I can see, to the west, valleys and homes and smaller hills in bright sunshine, but the hill I'm on is high and the stream will be in its shadow for some time. Cold is seeping into my feet and body, so I choose a path that runs directly back to the car. A cup of coffee at the doughnut shop down the road sounds good, and I can get a newspaper there, too. I can probably have the Sunday paper read before the rest of the family wakes up.

But, instead of driving away, I linger. I don't really want to leave just yet. A woodpecker has started hammering on a tree nearby. Cardinals have joined the song sparrows in full melody. A pair of mallard ducks is paddling about the shoreline. A kingfisher is perching on a branch over the water. Like me, he is waiting, watching.

I wander down the road a short distance, turn and watch the hilltop. It's cold enough to make me put my hood up again, but still I remain. I have a chance to see the sunrise for the third time this morning.

Then, just at the instant when the sun peeks across the hill, dozens of red-winged blackbirds in the cattails break loose with their noisy calls. A spontaneous, joyous din sweeps over the spot as sunlight floods the little valley. The birds seem to be celebrating. Hallelujah!

Maybe they greet each morning this way, but somehow it seems they know what day this is. I walk to the car; it's time to head for coffee and warmth. I feel strangely satisfied.

2

Where Spring Comes First

It's NOISY AND ACTIVE, a place alive. Color is there. And promise. Right now, the marsh is where I like to be. It's where I can watch spring develop.

Scientists say all life emerged from water at one time or another, and at this time of year I can believe it. In a way, it happens again every spring: life is being renewed, revived, reawakened.

Frogs and turtles, snakes and lizards all shake off months of hibernation and resume the business of living, which translates into searching for food and for mates, usually but not necessarily in that order. New life in all forms is being created. Already, some of the birds are pairing off. The wet places are where the first plants turn green, too, and where the first insects hatch, where microscopic organisms kick into gear.

It is the frogs, particularly the tiny tree frogs called spring peepers, that usually get me thinking about the marsh. The minute they awake, usually by mid-March, they start chanting, sending out mating calls so loudly I can hear them from inside the house. The peepers' cries create

a jumbled din, to be sure, but after the long winter silence, it is lovely music. It pulls me to the marsh.

On milder days and nights, the frogs' clamor is incredibly loud, yet they seem to be invisible. When disturbed by my approach, they abruptly shut up, but if I stand still for a moment, the noise quickly resumes. I then strain my eyes to see the tiny "singers" —no larger than a thumbnail—as they make their racket by billowing their throat sacs.

Occasionally, I see a snapping turtle emerge from the water. Heavily armored, slow and cranky, the snapper often drags strands of algae or some of the rotting vegetation as it crawls from the bog. Such a sight makes me think that maybe we're not so far removed from the age of dinosaurs after all.

Already pairs of mallard ducks are silently paddling around the marsh, getting ready to set up housekeeping. I try not to disturb them. If there is really anything "cute" in the wild, it's a brood of fuzzy little ducklings, and I'm hoping they'll nest here. The snapping turtle is hoping so, too,

I suppose; snappers can't resist duckling dinners.

Red-winged blackbirds are as boisterous as mallards are secretive. A flock screams a protest every time I arrive, whirling about just a few feet overhead. I've never been attacked by a redwing, but others have been. Redwings consider the marsh their private domain.

If I make my visit at dusk, and I'm lucky, I see and hear male woodcocks. These bizarre birds with chunky bodies and long bills put on quite a display for their lady friends by bobbing around in the damp meadow while uttering plaintive *peents* and spiraling up through the darkening sky on dizzying flights.

Twilight also gets other marsh critters moving. Muskrats seem to appear from nowhere. One moment, the water is still; the next, a long, silently rippling V reveals a muskrat swimming to or from the shallows, where tender green shoots are sprouting day by day.

Now that the frogs are awake, raccoons visit the bog regularly, and foxes, too, though they are cautious and I usually have to be content with seeing their tracks in the mud. Both coons and foxes come to hunt; they relish the ducks' eggs and babies. They know what I'm learning: the marsh is where spring's action begins.

3

Call of the Dove

THE SOUND HAS a poignancy to it, almost a sadness. It's been called more a wail than a song. That's why the mourning dove was given its name. But I love that sound. Especially now. Especially after a long winter.

In early spring, bird songs are commonplace. Some of the migrants—robins and red-winged blackbirds, in particular—are loud and loquacious. Birds that stayed here all winter in near-silence are also tuning up. Cardinals. Mockingbirds. Song sparrows. All celebrate spring's arrival with exuberance, their voices filled with cheerful sounds. They might not be into their full mating songs yet, but the whistles and trills and rambling phrases are chock-full of glad tidings. Happy noise, I call it.

Mourning doves are different. They must be just as relieved as the others to have survived another winter, just as grateful to perch out in the sunshine, but they cannot sing. They cannot make joyful sounds. When they call to each other, it is a low, soft *ooah-ooo-ooo*. More melancholy than musical. A hundred years ago, author-naturalist John Burroughs said the doves speak of "hopeless sorrow." I won't go that far, but I do think the name mourning dove is appropriate.

I never tire of that call. I've probably heard it every spring of my life, but it always stirs something deep inside. Maybe because it is so different. Maybe because it seems so sad. Maybe because it starts earlier in the year than most other bird songs. Maybe because it reminds me of good old days and good old places.

Years ago, as a farm boy who didn't know what creature was making that sound, I listened for it on spring evenings. Now I realize the doves

must have been in our apple trees, but the cooing seemed to come from well beyond the orchard, somewhere out in imagination. It was exotic, a call with images of far-away lands—what did I know?

Doves and their calls have been everywhere I've lived since. Small towns and suburbs and a New England village built on old farmland. Each spring, at least one pair of mourning doves would be nearby, close enough for that call to reach me through the chilling breezes of April twilight. They call at other times of day, too, but I'm around to hear them at dusk, and that's when the calls seem most appropriate. Let the happy birds greet the sunrise; doves say a solemn good-bye to the day.

I welcome other birds' spring songs, too, of course. I really look forward to some of them, and make a point of finding the singers. When I hear the first redwings chattering, I have to go find them. When I hear the excited song of a brown thrasher, or the sweet serenade of a wood thrush, I drop whatever I'm doing to search for the bird. But, for some reason, just hearing the dove is enough; there's no need to go find it.

I know that one is perched up on a wire or branch somewhere and cooing out its little heart just as fervently as the thrasher or the wood thrush. (A dove may lack musical talent but in spring, in mating season, it does not lack soul.) So I'll pause for a moment and listen.

I'll soon resume whatever I was doing—spading the garden, fussing over the fruit trees, wandering around the yard—but I'll feel a little more content. To me, the call is soothing and satisfying. A dove's voice may be sad; its message is not.

4

A Precious Secret

IT WAS SO EASY, I should have made the discovery years earlier. There I was, poking along, relishing the ambience of early spring—the sounds and sights and smells—and I walked right into a thick colony of trailing arbutus. Just like that. I wanted to celebrate.

Trailing arbutus is a wild flower, one of the earliest to bloom, and now becoming one of the hardest to find. These days, people who know where the arbutus grows usually keep such knowledge to themselves. It's a precious secret, like a great trout stream or a dependable place for morel mushrooms.

I'm that way, too, now. By late March or early April, I return to the spot where I found my first arbutus, but I've told only a select few about the flowers, and have shown even fewer where they grow. On my last visit, I found myself looking over my shoulder, making sure nobody was watching. Arbutus paranoia, I guess.

There was a time when the arbutus—also called mayflower—was so common it was regularly hawked on street corners around New England. Many people went out in spring and gathered up armloads of the tiny but fragrant pink blossoms and evergreen leaves just to decorate dining rooms and parlors. Everybody knew and revered them. "The flowers of God," gushed one 19th-century poet.

A hundred years ago, a naturalist called the arbutus "certainly the most poetic and best loved" of wild flowers. "So early, so lovely, so secretive there in the moss and dry leaves, so fragrant, tinged with the hues of youth and health, so hardy and homelike, it touches the heart as no other does."

An outdoors writer of another type and time wrote: "Best of all, among springtime perfumes, is a thin stream of fragrance which, once sampled, is never forgotten. For those of us who call New England home, no flower exudes so heady a brew, and none is so retiring as the arbutus."

But the arbutus was nearly loved to death. So many of the plants were uprooted, they gradually disappeared in many areas. When "development" came, with its bulldozers and stripped hillsides, more arbutus colonies perished. They do best in sandy soil at the edge of woods, where they are partially shaded—often hiding among the decaying fallen leaves of the previous autumn—and when the soil is disturbed or the protective trees removed, the arbutus suffers.

Now the plant is protected by law in many areas, but protection nearly came too late. And so the trailing arbutus (isn't that name far more imaginative than mayflower?) is almost a thing of the past. It's that difficult to find.

Another reason it is hard to find is the flower's size. An arbutus plant does trail, or creep, for several feet, but the individual blossoms are barely half an inch across. With them hugging the ground, they're easily overlooked.

That's also a reason why it took so long for me to find them. At this time of year, with so much happening, I tend to look up, at the swallows and butterflies and unfurling leaves.

However, now that I know where the arbutus is, I take at least one walk each April that gets me down there in the dirt. I, too, have come to revel in the fragrance that inspired the old poets.

But don't ask me for directions.

5

The Dependable Migrants

EACH DAY NOW, the volume is turned up another notch. More bird song because there are more birds. The travelers are drifting in. Soon they'll be arriving in a steady stream, reviving not only a joyousness about the countryside but also some age-old questions.

To many of the questions, we have no answers, as yet. How does a young catbird that never migrated find its way back to the same thicket in which it was hatched the summer before? How does a tiny humming-bird travel the thousands of miles to Central America and back without falling prey to some hawk—and how does it go that far without wearing out? How does a thrush flying up the East Coast know that this little wood lot is the place for it to stop and build a nest?

But even beyond the how of migration, which has been studied a great deal by scientists, the question that occurs to me each spring is, Why? Why do these birds come back here? Why is the kingfisher back at my favorite little pond—the lakes down south haven't run out of fish, have they? Why will the oriole be hanging its pouchlike nest along the river again—aren't there enough tall trees in Central America? Why do the swallows come back—do our mosquitoes taste better than those in the south? Why will the bobolinks insist on trying to find hayfields around here, where there are fewer each year, when they could fly less and find more elsewhere?

Maybe there is no need to look for the answers. Maybe we should just cherish the birds and their songs while we have the chance.

Scientists tell us the songs are simply part of courtship rituals, instinct without emotion. But I find that hard to believe. Watch a song sparrow

or yellow warbler as it belts out its song. Each puts so much of itself into the song that its body trembles. Is such heartfelt effort necessary to fill obligations of instinct? The birds seem to be singing for themselves, not for prospective mates. And nobody can tell me a brown thrasher has no emotion. That bird's song has so much exuberance, so much ecstasy, that I firmly believe the thrasher sings just because spring has arrived and the sun is shining and it feels good to be alive.

I almost added another reason for the thrasher's enthusiasm: that it is glad to be home. But that brings up another question about the migrants. What is home? Is it here, where they mate and nest and hatch their young? Or is home where they spend the winter months? For many of our birds, the stay here is relatively short, certainly less than half the year. Some shorebirds don't arrive until May and are gone by mid-August. Even the songbirds that are streaming in now will be leaving by September. That gives them more time in their winter quarters and on the road than where they nest. So which place should be considered home?

It doesn't matter, I suppose. Most people who delight in having birds around are going to think of their place as the birds' home, whether the birds stay for four months or eight months. I feel that way, too. If a bluebird family uses one of my birdhouses, that is its home, even if the occupancy lasts only a month. If a wren builds a nest in one of the shrubs, my yard will become its home, and I'll welcome it back next spring, even though it spends most of the year elsewhere.

Actually, scientists have made much progress in figuring out migration. At one time, people thought birds hibernated in winter, like woodchucks and turtles and frogs and various insects; now we know where most of the birds go, and even how they navigate. We know they find directions by the sun and stars and certain landmarks. We know about flyways and migration patterns. We can predict which birds will come back first, and the approximate dates of arrival. We know how much havoc storms can play with migration. We know that many of the birds that leave here in fall do not make it all the way to winter quarters, and many more do not survive the journey back.

We're less certain about the reasons. Supposedly, many of our birds originated in the tropics, expanded their ranges northward after the Ice Age and now return south out of habit. That would make the south "home" then, wouldn't it? Other theories on the why of migration include food supply and living space, and how various climates affect fertility. The subject is both fascinating and baffling. But migration is something to ponder at night, or on stormy days, or maybe during long winter evenings in front of the fireplace. Not on sparkling April mornings.

No, right now—when a wren or warbler or thrasher erupts into full song, or a kingfisher cuts loose with its rattling cry, or a thrush sends its serenade from the forest—there is no reason to ask why they have returned. It seems more appropriate to simply welcome them back, and enjoy the music.

6

Fish are an Excuse

By THE TIME the sun burns away the dawn mist, the fishermen have already been at the pond for an hour or so. It's cold and damp, and the fish aren't cooperating, but there is no place these people would rather be.

It's April, and that means it's fishing season. They would like to catch fish, of course; there is still something electric about the sudden strike and the tug on the line. But whether they land any fish or not, April fishermen are renewing an acquaintance with the mist and the dew-laden twigs and the dawn birdsong. With the morning itself. It's been too long. Being out there as the day begins stirs something deep inside these men, something they find hard to put into words. They would feel self-conscious about getting up this early just to enjoy the dawn, so they go fishing.

I don't know if it's ever been proven that fish bite more readily at dawn, but every single fisherman I know insists that is the case. He wouldn't trade two hours of fishing before breakfast for four hours in the afternoon. Even if he caught the same number of fish. There is a magic about the dawn that is lost to the late-riser.

By afternoon, the fog is gone. The dew has vanished. The red-winged blackbirds aren't quite as loud or boisterous as they were at sunrise. The kingfisher that rattled away at the fisherman's approach in the morning is more subdued, less conspicuous. The mallard hen that may already be shepherding a brood of ducklings has returned to her nest. Perhaps the bass and trout react no differently, but the aware fisherman knows he has missed a major part of the experience.

In most cases, a boy learns fishing from his father. Being allowed to join Dad on a dawn trip to the pond is a significant milestone in a great many lives, and it is a wise man who makes fishing more than a matter of catching fish. The man who quietly points out the kingfisher to his son, the father who mentions the raccoon tracks in the shoreline mud, gives his boy a richer appreciation of the pond than one who only details which lure to use and where the trout are most likely to be hiding.

I, too, first went fishing with my father, but it is not the fish that I remember. Dad was the old-fashioned fisherman; all he needed was a cane pole, a line, a cork, a sinker and a hook. And a can of worms. And patience. He would sit on the bank and wait for the fish. While he waited, he would tell me about the nearby trees and flowers, about the gangling blue herons that stalked the shallows, about the muskrats that occasionally swam across our stream. It never mattered to me whether we caught fish; I came back from each trip excited over new discoveries.

Because there seemed so many things more interesting than fish, I was not a good fisherman. I lacked Dad's patience. When I went five minutes without a bite, I'd put down my pole and wander off. I'd go looking for the oriole nest above the stream, or I'd search for the dogwood trees my father had mentioned, or I'd go see if I could find the tree where he had carved his initials 35 years earlier. I'd search for the first blooming violets and I would lie on the banks and stare down into the water, trying to see crayfish. I could spend hours prowling each gravel bar looking for arrowheads. I never found one, but that didn't stop me from hoping. Eventually, I left the fishing pole at home when I went roaming along the stream.

Now I'm being reintroduced to fishing by my own sons, who somehow picked up most of their expertise on their own. They use spinning reels instead of cane poles, Hula Poppers and Jittersticks and other fancy artificial lures instead of worms—most of the time—and they've never seen a cork bobber. But the things that really matter haven't changed. They catch more fish than I did at their age—for that matter, they catch more than I do now—but the blue herons are still the same. So are the muskrats and the violets and the dogwood trees.

They tell me where the bass are lurking; I tell them about lily pads and pickerel weeds. They show me how to drop their plugs under overhanging branches; I try to show them which backwaters are most likely to have muskrat lodges. They talk about the differences between bluegills and pumpkinseeds; I point out the differences between a downy woodpecker and a hairy woodpecker. We have a great time.

There is the usual generation gap, I suppose, with different tastes in music and clothes, different values and different goals. But we are finding that we still can share a great deal. All three of us like seeing a mama mallard paddling about with a dozen ducklings. We like listening to the cry of the kingfisher. We enjoy seeing the mist rise from a quiet pond. We find beauty in dew sparkling in the sunshine. In short, we relish being out there when a new day is created. So we go fishing.

7

Profane and Profound

THERE ARE FLOWERS—wild flowers—growing on our old neighbor's grave. Nothing could be more fitting.

My wife and I stand there, bundled up against the cold wind that sweeps across that little hillside cemetery, and say almost in unison: "He would have liked it this way."

It is somehow completely appropriate that the flowers are small and unpretentious—Bettie identifies them as moss phlox—because the old man was small and unpretentious. He was what he was, for better or worse. To some people, he was crude and archaic, a man out of step with the times. To me, he was fascinating, a fount of knowledge about a New England I never knew.

He was already an old man, beyond ordinary retirement age, when we met him; but he was going full speed. He was a carpenter by trade; but he preferred hunting, fishing, trapping and tending his beehives and huge gardens. He was earthy, in more ways than one; but I found him profound as well as profane.

There was something of the philosopher about him, and many of the predictions he made concerning the environment many years ago have come to pass. He was opinionated on most subjects—from religion and politics to baseball and cars—but I usually steered the conversation back to the woods and waters and wild creatures, if I could. They were his world.

Those in our neighborhood who remember him at all—he had moved away more than ten years before he died—probably recall the front porch that was always flanked by wooden rain barrels. On the long porch, throughout the year, would be the fruits of his labor, so to speak. There might be raccoon or fox carcasses, waiting to be skinned. Or a pair of partridges that he hadn't gotten around to cleaning. Or a string of horned pout. Or buckets of blueberries or raspberries. Or perhaps a live snapping turtle that a friend had caught and dropped off. Or a tub of honeycombs from his hives. Or large piles of cabbages or turnips or corn from his garden. And potatoes; always potatoes.

It's easy to think of a man who leaves dead animals on his porch as crude, but there was another side to him that casual acquaintances seldom saw. He fed birds all winter—was one of the first to do that. He knew the Latin names of nearly every wild flower in the woods and marshes, and kept a fantastic terrarium of wild plants in his kitchen. He loved providing live salamanders and frogs to any schoolchildren who asked for them. And eventually I learned that he gave away bushels of vegetables every year.

What he gave me I valued far more than sweet corn or potatoes. His stories of New England winters 70 and 80 years ago, and what our town was like before World War II—in fact, before World War I—were fascinating, even though I suspected considerable exaggeration. As a boy, he helped his grandfather run a trap line along a stream now buried beneath a reservoir. They trapped minks, otters, muskrats, foxes, raccoons and skunks.

He knew a time and place that had vanished by my arrival. He remembered when woodcocks were so thick he supplied several hotels and restaurants with the birds, shooting them with loads of turnip seeds, instead of buckshot, to protect the meat. (He said hotel managers suggested substituting robins when woodcocks became scarce.) He told me of the day he caught 13 partridges in horsehair snares; the snares, installed in brush barriers, never missed, he said. He showed me how the snares were made, but I've forgotten by now. I haven't forgotten the stories.

When he moved away, to spend his final years with relatives, I lost touch with him. I hadn't even thought of him for a long time before I saw his death notice in the paper, and it was another eight months or so before my wife and I, on the spur of the moment, went looking for his grave.

The stone is austere, noting nothing more than his name, date of birth and date of death. Just like almost all the other stones in the cemetery.

But his is the only grave I see with wild flowers growing on it. In a way, the tiny flowers bring back more memories of my old friend than a name chiseled in stone. He probably was crude, and perhaps was out of step with the times; but I'll always be glad I knew him.

8

Plowing

SPRING BRINGS DIFFERENT things to mind for different people. To some, it's golf and baseball. To others, it's crocuses and tulips. Or robins and red-winged blackbirds. Or fishing and canoeing. Maybe even mud and mosquitoes.

Well, spring means all of those things, but another symbol of the season also pops into my head each year at this time: plowing.

It's strange how certain things stay with you over the years. I've been off the farm for more than half of my life, but I still cannot think of spring without thinking of plowing. Maybe that's because plowing was one of the few chores I actually enjoyed—mowing and raking hay were the others—and maybe because my parents occasionally let me skip school at plowing time.

All farm work automatically became more attractive if it meant staying home from school, although I remember stressing the importance of education on days when my team had baseball games. But plowing was more than getting away from places I didn't want to be; it was going toward something I knew even then was special. It was a way of basking in the still-unfamiliar warmth of early-spring sunshine. It was feeling part of the awakening process that comes to the land each spring.

As I plowed, I watched the redwings flying around me, trying to drown out the tractor's clattering with their chatter. I noticed how the robins followed the plow, ready to pounce on uncovered worms. I liked the looks of a freshly plowed field, so clean and ready, particularly if the ground being turned under had been drab all winter with severed cornstalks or some other stubble left over from a vanished harvest—from a season that suddenly seemed long ago.

But best of all was—and is—the smell. There is a fragrance to newly turned soil that is hard to describe. It is earthy, elemental. It is warm and moist. To farmers, to those people who live on and with the land, it is an aroma as sweet as any flower's, as refreshing as any tonic's. It is the smell of promise, of hope, of growth. It is the smell of spring.

My father and I used to disagree on plowing procedures. Like many farmers all over the country, he liked plowing up the fields in fall, almost as soon as the corn or soybeans or other crops were taken off. He said turning under the stubble helped rebuild the soil over the winter, and having the fields plowed gave him a head start on chores once spring came. I suppose he was right on both points, but I usually mentioned the drawbacks, particularly how much of the plowed topsoil we'd lose to the howling winds during the winter. Snow would be swept off the fields by the wind, and where it piled up along fences it would soon be turned dark by bits of soil stripped off by succeeding gales.

It was a good argument—one I would use again today—but there was another point to my reasoning. To me, plowing was meant to be done in spring if for no other reason than to start a new growing season at its beginning. By opening the soil, releasing all the fragrances and optimism that go with springtime on the farm, we were putting ourselves in the

right frame of mind for the planting and fertilizing and cultivating that followed, all the way to the eventual harvesting. I remember an old farmer who thought as I did telling me how spring plowing "prepares the land while preparing the man."

Even in these difficult times for farmers, it is hard not to feel a certain optimism when getting ready for a new season. When freshly plowed, each field carries the promise of bounty. That's one of the great things about farming. In April, you can expect every seed that is put in the ground to germinate, every one to grow tall and straight, every one to mature and produce a profitable harvest. This year, there will be enough rain, enough sunshine, and no hail storms. This year, everything will be perfect. The stuff of dreams, you say? Sure it is, but maybe you have to be a bit of a dreamer to be a farmer, and if you can't dream in early spring, when can you?

These days, my "farm" is a sandy, rock-lined, often weedy vegetable garden, which I manage to shrink a little each year. I've discovered I'm not a very good gardener, mainly because I don't really care if green beans and peppers and squashes ever grow. I'm not going to eat them, anyway. I even find it hard to stay interested in the vegetables I do like; there's not much challenge to growing carrots or radishes or even tomatoes. So by July my wife usually winds up doing the weeding and watering.

But I still do the plowing each spring, although now it is usually with a spade rather than a tractor. I still want to turn over the ground, to see and smell and feel the new season opening at my feet. Spring would arrive, I suppose, even if I skipped this ritual—but I don't want to miss it. It is important to me. I don't want to forget that while people may believe the earth belongs to them, they also belong to the earth.

9

May

ONE OF THESE YEARS, I'm going to spend this whole month roaming around the fields and woods and waters. Maybe then I'll be able to keep up with the happenings of May, and maybe I'll be able to stay out of trouble.

I've always found May too tantalizing, too tempting. It leads me astray. I want to be out there when the brown thrasher is singing; I want to walk among the wildflowers and apple blossoms. Instead, like so many in our modern, tightly structured world, I'm supposed to be inside during the day. Duty calls us one way; the heart and mind pull us in another direction.

Sometimes, May and the thrasher and the sunshine win. It happened so often back in high school that I nearly didn't reach graduation. I'd go to class in the morning with the best of intentions. But the windows would be open, and the breeze would carry the fragrance of the lilac blossoms just outside, and I'd start thinking about the turtles sunning themselves and the robins in their new nests. By lunch break, my resistance would be gone, and so was I.

My school was right beside a stream, and it was easy in those days to slip away into the shoreline trees. I'd spend the afternoon among the creatures of that stream, the turtles and frogs, the ducks and herons, the muskrats and chipmunks. I'd start roaming, wandering from one discovery to another, and soon find myself a mile or two from school.

I remember listening, on one of those stolen afternoons, to the most exuberant songbird I had ever heard. It was at the very top of a 12- or 15-foot shrub, head straight up, singing so loudly and fervently its entire body was trembling. I lingered so long I missed my bus and had to walk home—a frequent occurrence—but I didn't mind at all. I don't recall what the punishment was, but I'm sure I considered the day worth any price. That was my first brown thrasher, and to this day I've never heard a bird celebrate spring with more down-to-the-soul enthusiasm. It lured me away to other afternoons and more penalties—teachers and parents just didn't understand—because that song said just exactly what I felt.

Adulthood has made me only slightly more responsible. Fortunately, for job security, I can no longer smell the lilacs from my desk, but in a way that only makes me yearn all the more to be beyond walls and windows. Just knowing spring is out there and not being able to participate in it can be little short of torture. Snippets of time in the evenings and weekends are not enough.

Wouldn't it be great to be free to roam at will? Men like John Muir and Henry David Thoreau did it. They successfully rebelled against routine and wandered to their hearts' content. They roamed throughout the year; I'd be satisfied with just May, and perhaps October, the other time when walls become prisons. Just two months out of 12; that doesn't seem to be asking so much.

I don't think it would be hard to fill the days. Right now, I want to canoe every stream, fish every pond, climb every hillside, walk every trail. They all call to me as I go by: siren songs that are nearly irresistible in May.

I'd go looking for the kingfisher's nest—I've never found one—and I'd see if the bluebirds have returned to the old pasture. I'd see if the frogs' eggs have hatched yet in the woodland pools and if the wild strawberries are beginning to blossom.

Are the ladyslippers blooming yet? How about the arbutus and the mayapples? I'd make my yearly pilgrimage to an ancient orchard, to see if the abandoned apple trees will blossom one more time. I'd look for baby squirrels and I'd listen to the meadowlark's song and I'd sit on a rocky ledge somewhere and drowse in the sunshine.

Come to think of it, I'd be doing many of the same things I did on those afternoons when I was supposed to be studying geometry and world history. Either I never grew up, or May makes me feel that I didn't.

Let's start a campaign to have the entire month declared a holiday, or holimonth. We wait so long for spring to come, surely we should have a chance to enjoy it. Would commerce and industry and education really collapse if we spent a few weeks biking and sailing and golfing and fishing and playing tennis? Maybe we need more Muirs and Thoreaus; maybe they had the right way to approach life.

Anyway, I still hope to have my May without obligations some year. I presume the thrashers and the lilacs will still be out there. And I'm no longer worried about missing the bus.

10

Welcome Back

THE GOOSE HUNCHES down low on her nest, trying to hide from us. She keeps her body perfectly still, but cannot resist following our movements with her head. Even as we float past she watches us, ever on guard, her long neck twisted so that she can see over her shoulder.

We're curious about the nest but don't want to disturb the goose, so we circle the tiny island once, and then paddle away. It's obvious she's incubating eggs, and scaring her off the nest could be harmful; if the eggs get cold, they might not hatch. But we don't need to get closer; just knowing the nest is there is enough.

It wasn't so long ago that it was unlikely we would see wild geese nesting in southern New England. Commonly called Canada geese, they were dwindling in numbers, and about the only ones we'd see were the high-flying flocks that crossed overhead in spring and fall, and those that lingered in the salt marshes in winter.

Times change, though, and the big geese are among the birds that are thriving these days. Not only are we seeing far more wild geese, but many of them are living here. Numerous ponds have stable goose populations now, whether a pair of geese or a small flock, and it's not uncommon to see large numbers grazing in fields and on golf courses, like so many sheep.

Wildlife people say these year-round geese are descendants of non-migrant birds that lived here years ago, tough geese that moved out only in the most severe weather, and then only as far as necessary. The number of those birds decreased sharply for a while, but now the geese are reproducing rapidly.

In fact, geese are becoming so abundant in parts of the Northeast that they're considered pests, not only for their devouring of grass, grain, and other plant life, but also for the mess they make wherever they gather. Hunting seasons are being extended just to control these permanent-resident birds.

If I owned a fairway fouled by geese, or had a wheat field destroyed by their daily raids, I'd complain too. But I don't, so I'm enjoying the return of the geese.

To me, there are few sights as exhilarating as a flock of wild geese arrowing through the sky in February and March, announcing the impending arrival of spring. Similarly, their appearance in October is both poignant and ominous, symbolic of the glories of autumn and the onset of winter. And for sheer primal wildness, what sounds can rival the geese's calling through the fog and darkness as they travel their thousands of miles each way each year?

That our geese don't fly as far makes little difference. They still honk plaintively when on the wing. They still arrange themselves in that distinctive V when a flock gets up in the sky. They still stir deep inside many of us the urge to wander, to cross the endless horizons.

So I go with my son to check the nest he found on the miniature island—the first goose nest we've seen on this pond.

I'm not thinking "pest" as I watch the goose. I'm thinking how exciting it is to see geese —even just a pair of them—dropping out of the sky. I'm thinking of all the sights and sounds of wild geese, and how they've touched generations of us earth-bound humans.

I find myself saying "Welcome" to the goose. "Welcome and good luck."

11

Reaping the Memories

HE STOOD AT the shore and looked. Before him was a flooded marsh, the product of the beaver dam we had just passed. Beside him was the beavers' lodge, a huge mound of mud and sticks. Scattered around him were stumps, the stumps with the distinctive cone-shaped tops that remain when beavers have gnawed off trees.

The man was gazing at one of the more active beaver ponds in Rhode Island, but I had a feeling his mind was racing back over the years, to other ponds and other times. He looked around in silence for many long moments, then finally turned and thanked me for bringing him to the spot. And started telling stories.

He told of large beaver colonies in the area of Maine where he'd spent his boyhood. He recalled working trap lines at one stage of his life, and at another, feeding willow twigs to a beaver for a month. He spoke of grueling snowshoe treks and plunges into icy streams, of long-ago winters and long-gone friends who shared his adventures.

I soaked it up. Every word. Old-timers like this man fascinate me, those who enjoyed their youth, those who spent time roaming the back country. They knew another New England, a place and time I think I would have loved. Their portrayals of those days are so much more alive than anything I've read in books. If occasionally they embellish a fact or two, well, that's okay. I think they're entitled.

This man, a neighbor and friend of long standing, is about 75, maybe older; I've never asked. His arms and legs don't work as well as they once did. The steps are slow and unsteady; a cane is necessary. But the mind is sharp, the memory clear. With those strengths, and a delightful wit,

he's a natural storyteller.

And he has hundreds of stories. Fishing stories. Flying stories. Canoing stories. Camping stories. Moose stories. Bear stories. Blizzard stories. And, I learned that day, beaver stories. He tells each with flair and humor, dramatic gestures and colorful epithets.

Bettie and I had stopped at the pond a few days earlier, and when we noticed how much activity had taken place recently, and how near the road the beaver lodge and dam were, she suggested inviting the man and his wife to go there with us. He'd be able to see the beavers' handiwork without a long hike; with luck, he might even see a beaver swimming. He'd love that.

We didn't see any beavers when we went, but that hardly mattered. The man said he hadn't visited a beaver pond in years, and he seemed perfectly satisfied just to be there. Between stories, he offered insights. This colony was getting too big for the food available, he said, noting that the beavers had felled maples and oaks and even gnawed a pine or two—not their favorite foods. He was surprised that they had even chosen an area without willows and " popples" (poplars), the trees that they like. He speculated that there were probably youngsters in the lodge at the time we visited, and predicted we'd find another lodge or two if we continued upstream.

We lingered, sometimes talking, sometimes just looking, for quite a while. When we finally left, our friend thanked us again, saying that this trip was a treat.

Thanks were not necessary. It was a treat for us, too. On outings with people like that man and woman, we always get far more than we give. Always.

12

Awaiting the Orioles

THIS YEAR, I'm going to pay close attention. This year, I'm going to check out the tall trees along the river as often as possible. This year, I'm not going to wait until fall to see an oriole nest.

In fact, I plan to watch an oriole weave its unique pouch. I might even cheat a little bit.

Orioles are arriving from the South right now—Mother's Day is often considered the target date for their return—and in a matter of days the females will begin gathering material for those nests. Maybe if I leave some gaudy yarn—orange or red or yellow—lying around, the birds will take it along with the other fibers they use. A bit of color in the nests might make them easier to find.

I don't think the orioles would mind using bright yarn. They seem to change with the times rather well. For one thing, they've had their name changed. For many, many years, they were known as Baltimore orioles—long before there was a baseball

team by that name. Supposedly, it's because their colors, a spectacular orange set off by black and white, were the family colors of the Calverts, one of whom was Lord Baltimore. A few years ago, the birding fraternity changed the birds to northern orioles—I can't remember why—at a time when many bird names were altered. I suppose it makes no difference to the birds, but I've resisted the changes. I may not say "Baltimore orioles" much these days, but I refuse to say "northern orioles." They're simply orioles to me now, even though there is another, less common variety, the orchard oriole. (Now that's a picturesque name. Wonder how long before it, too, is changed.)

Anyway, there was a time when orioles used a lot of horsehair in stringing together the nests that they hung at the tips of branches high in elm trees. New England villages were lined with elms in those days, and orioles were a familiar sight. Now most of the elms are gone and so are many of the horses. The orioles don't seem unduly affected; they've merely improvised.

They nest in maples and sycamores and other trees now, and don't insist on being quite as high as before. That should make nest building easier to watch, but the birds have retreated from the villages for the most part, preferring to live along streams and ponds, where they are less likely to be disturbed. Every autumn, after the leaves are gone, I find half a dozen oriole nests in a mile stretch along one particular river, each one suspended over the water, each one undetected while it was occupied. Seeing them sway in the wind during the winter is significant—they're a link between the seasons, a reminder of the summer that was and a promise of the spring that will be—but I always feel a twinge of regret over not noticing the orioles more while they were here.

So I'm going to put out some bright yarn, and then check the trees more closely over the next month or so. I'd love to be able to watch one of these nests being woven. I never have.

The less flamboyant female does all the work—the male is too busy singing to help. She loops and pushes and pulls the nesting materials together, one piece at a time, until she has a pouch about eight inches long. All sorts of material go into the nests. Much of it is vegetable fiber, usually taken from decaying plants from the previous year. The tough white stuff inside old milkweed stems is one favorite. Grasses, grapevine bark and strips of other plant fibers are used, too. The modern orioles use string, fishline and odd pieces of yarn and cloth as well.

An oriole nest is the original cradle in the treetop, and when the wind blows, the cradle does rock. But the orioles pick boughs that seldom break, and the pouch, though appearing fragile, is not only strong enough to withstand the storms of summer, but usually lasts through most of the following winter as well.

I've already marked the trees where nests hung last year, and will be keeping particularly close watch on them because orioles often do return to the same trees. I'll try not to be too distracted by the male's sweet music and brilliant colors—although ignoring him is not easy—and to pay more attention to the female's activities. If I watch what she does and where she goes, I should be able to see a nest built.

The plan is all ready. This could be the year.

13

The Harvest of Blossoms

TWICE BLESSED. That's what a person is when he grows his own fruit. Just as people who cut their own firewood are twice warmed—once when they saw the logs and then when they burn them—those who have fruit trees are doubly rewarded. Not only do they get all those good things to eat in summer and fall, but they also get a world of blossoms each spring.

There are times—often, in my case—when the blossoms are even better than the fruit. It's not that I don't care about eating; it's just that blossoms are more dependable, and less work. Also, I don't have to own the trees to enjoy the blossoms. I can drive or walk by any orchard in spring and help myself to the beauty and fragrance. There might be a problem if I similarly helped myself to the peaches and apples.

I have planted some fruit trees in the yard: two peaches, two plums, two apples and one cherry. We've been getting peaches for a few years, but we're still waiting for the other trees to mature.

So, for now, I have to buy my fruit, and I go on reaping my harvest of blossom enjoyment from other people's trees. That's rather easy in my part of the state, because there are still numerous orchards around. The pink and white blossoms can be seen from a distance, gleaming in the sunshine, and the subtle but sweet aromas likewise extend beyond the stone walls.

Early May is apple-blossom time. In most years pears bloom first, then peaches and plums — all weeks before the apples. The reason for the early blossomings seems to go beyond competition for the pollination services of the bees. If the peaches, pears and plums bloomed at the same time as the apples, there would be another form of competition—for appreciation. An apple orchard in full bloom can be rather overwhelming.

Taken as individuals, the peach blossoms might be the loveliest. They are a soft pink with a crimson center, reminding me of a miniature wild rose. Peach twigs in flower are pretty enough to clip and put in a vase.

Both the pear and the plum blossoms are basically white, and tiny. If seen alone they would be inconspicuous, but they come in clusters—usually enough so that the trees seem gowned in white.

Yet, much as I like the other blossoms, when the apple display begins I know the peaches and pears and plums were only opening acts. This is when I wish I had my own orchard—even more than at picking time. I would choose an orchard of old varieties, the kind now abandoned in most of New England. Those trees don't produce the quality of apples demanded by today's commercial growers, but in May I'm not thinking of apples; the old varieties seem to have larger, even more colorful blossoms than the modern trees.

But walking through any apple orchard in blossom time can be like strolling through a bouquet. The senses are caressed, and not just those of sight and smell. There is the excited murmur of a million bees to listen to, and the fresh new grass and leaves, as well as the silky petals, to touch.

There is also something more. A blossoming apple orchard has a special aura: all around are feelings of satisfaction and anticipation. Here is proof that spring has reached its pinnacle, and promise of the bounty to come. When people close to their land are surrounded by apple blossoms, they know they have the best that this season can offer.

14

The Last Dinosaurs

WE SWING THE canoe around a wooded point of land and glide into a shallow, muddy backwater. This spot is our goal. Here, we can drift back millions of years. Here, we can almost always count on finding snapping turtles.

The sun is beating down. The surrounding trees and high banks prevent any breeze from reaching us. Here, the day's heat is amplified. Here, it feels like mid-summer. A perfect spot for snappers.

We paddle as quietly as possible, floating slowly toward the weeds and brush at the end of this inlet. Insects of a hundred varieties swirl around us. Frogs cry out as they plop into the water. A kingfisher rattles from an overhead branch. It is announcing our arrival. I wonder if the snapping turtles care.

Numerous painted turtles are sunning themselves on logs, their shells gleaming in the sunshine. As we approach, watching them slide, one by one, out of sight, we only half-notice a greenish boulder in the water until we're just a few feet away. Hey, that's it, we say together. That's a snapping turtle.

Snapping turtles are among those creatures I enjoy meeting as long as it's on my terms. I don't want to be surprised by a snapper, to come face to face with one unexpectedly. They're a little too ugly, too unnerving, for that.

It still happens, of course. Each year I'll run across one or two while I'm out walking. Usually, it's about this time of year, when females leave the water to lay their eggs. And if we meet on a path, guess which of us yields the right of way.

Snappers are not timid. They're tough customers—armor plating, long claws, hooked beaks—and they know it. They will readily charge anything that bothers them. If my dog is along when I find a snapper, I quickly change directions and drag Rusty with me. A dog is no match for a snapper.

When the eggs hatch, the babies instinctively head for water, and even a baby only a couple of inches long has its parents' sour disposition. I've been attacked by such tiny beasts. It's almost funny to see a baby snapper hiss and lunge and try to sink its beak into something hundreds of times larger, but the little tank is deadly serious. And it wouldn't be funny if that beak caught bare skin.

I've never been hurt by a snapper, but they've given me a couple of memorable frights. Once, as a kid wading in a muddy stream we used as a swimming hole, I stepped on a large submerged rock, which started moving. It didn't take long to figure out that rock was no rock. Another time I reached into the water beneath a log to pull out one of my father's turtle lines, and came up dragging a 15-pound snapper by the tail. I could just as easily have grabbed the other end.

The snapper's beak is a powerful weapon. A large turtle has a biting force figured at more than 400 pounds per square inch. And once it grabs something, it simply won't let go. Those who butcher snappers often provoke them into grasping sticks; then, by pulling on the sticks, they can extend the turtles' necks far enough for decapitation. Even death doesn't end the snapper's bite. Stories abound of severed heads continuing to bite for hours. Yes, you better know what you're doing when you mess with a snapper.

Still, the turtles fascinate me for some reason. Maybe it's because they look like—and are—throwbacks to the dinosaur era. Maybe it's because they're so antisocial, such loners. Maybe it's because of their apparent invincibility, their get-out-of-my-way arrogance.

Whatever the reason, I'll take the canoe out a few times each spring specifically to see how the snappers are faring. It's a little safer from a canoe and usually easier to slip up close to them unnoticed.

My son has never forgotten the time we came upon two huge males fighting in shallow water. They were so engrossed in combat we floated right up to them and actually bumped them before they noticed us. Even then, they snapped at each other a few more times before diving, in opposite directions, toward the unseen bottom.

Many times we've seen the big snappers drowsing in the sunshine, half in and half out of water, and mistaking them for boulders isn't so unusual. It happens most of the time. When their shells are dried, they do indeed resemble rough, algae-covered fieldstone.

Best places to find snappers are sluggish streams and languid ponds. Such sites seem to have other slow-moving creatures, and that's what the turtles live on, along with plant material. They catch some fish, some frogs, some crayfish, an occasional duckling, other turtles—virtually anything, alive or dead, suits the snappers' taste. Those who trap snappers—they make good soup—use bits of smelly carcasses as bait, and the smellier the better, because snappers find much of their food by following their noses. If they can reach adulthood, and avoid people, snappers may grow to more than 50 pounds and live for decades. Raccoons, foxes and other animals routinely dig up the eggs, but almost no wild animals will tangle with adult snappers. Animals aren't dumb.

We float up to the motionless snapper. It's a big one, probably 25 pounds or more. The shell has to be at least 18 inches across. We approach from its side; we can see both the head, held right at the water's surface, and the tail, which droops just below the surface.

Without a word, we spend several moments just looking over this monster, so little changed in the millions of years since its ancestors first lumbered through bogs and swam in ponds. From our modern-day, aluminum canoe we are staring back across the centuries at something that knew the Mesozoic Era, the time of dinosaurs.

It is aware of us, I'm sure, but tries to ignore us. We keep a few feet away, and silently marvel at that fearsome head, with its tiny, unblinking eyes. We note the rough shell, never large enough for the head to be withdrawn all the way in, as smaller turtles do. We look over the thick, pointed tail with its row of raised, prehistoric bumps down the spine.

Finally, it tires of us and pushes forward with a thrust of its powerful legs. It is quickly into deeper water and sinks out of sight, sliding into the murky depths. We watch clouds of mud rise in the water, and then settle again. The snapper has vanished, but it will be back. It will be here long after we are gone.

15

Whippoorwill

Any night now, I expect to hear the whippoorwill. This is about the time of year when it starts calling from the darkness. And I'm looking forward to hearing it again, despite last year.

I've always liked whippoorwills—there's an intriguing aura around a bird that almost nobody ever sees—but there were times last summer when I thought I would never want to hear another one.

Whippoorwills just don't know when to shut up.

Whippoorwills are drab, funny-looking birds with whiskers. They sleep all day and spend their nights gobbling up insects. When they're courting, in May and June, they also do a lot of whistling to each other. They whistle, and whistle, and whistle. On and on and on. I don't know when they find time to eat.

The call—some people call it a song, but I don't—can be stirring, even fascinating. For a while. It has a primal sound to it, ancient and wild and unique. If you've never heard it before, it can be eerie, bringing impressions of something strange and possibly sinister lurking in the night. But to those who know what it is, the whippoorwill's call says an old friend is back. It reminds the listener of days of youth, when evenings were spent out-

doors, on the porch, instead of indoors, parked in front of a television set.

However, there are also times when the call can be irritating. The three-syllable whistle, vaguely translated by the imaginative as *whip-poor-will*, sometimes continues for hours. Even a whippoorwill that doesn't get an answer will keep on whistling, with hardly a pause for breath, half of the night. Get two of them challenging each other from opposite sides of a valley, and you may never get to sleep.

That's the way it was last summer. My boys and I spent several weeks roaming around the country, camping out each night in seemingly quiet forest settings. There were whippoorwills at nearly every site. We never saw them, of course, but we heard them almost every night, almost all night. The first few nights we were delighted, because like most people we don't normally spend our nights in the woods, and had not heard the calls much in recent years.

But as the trip wore on, it became less than exciting to hear the birds whistle all night. It got to the point where I considered firing a shoe into the darkness, to scare them away, just as people supposedly hurl objects out windows at cats squalling in the backyard. A whippoorwill's call is far easier on the ears than a lovesick cat's yowling, but it still loses some of its enchantment after a couple of hours.

There were some nights when we slept very little.

Now, a year later, I'm ready to hear the whippoorwill call again. Partly because I really do like the sound, and partly because I don't like most night-flying insects.

Like their city cousins, the nighthawks, whippoorwills are almost flying vacuum cleaners when it comes to devouring bugs. They have wide mouths, surrounded by whiskerlike fringes, and cruise about collecting mosquitoes, gnats and moths.

They do most of their hunting over woods clearings, meadows and pastures, but often they venture close to rural homes—and camps—as they pursue insects that are attracted to lights. Besides the countless mosquitoes, gnats and standard moths the whippoorwills eat, they also feed on gypsy moths. That would make them ideal neighbors . . . if they just knew when to shut up.

For all the whippoorwills I've listened to over the years, I recall seeing only one, and that was by luck. I was tramping through a thick woods when I came close to stepping on one. It flew up to a low branch in an oak, perched just long enough for me to get a good look, and then disappeared into the brush.

There have been a few other times, while driving along country roads at night, when I've thought I glimpsed whippoorwills in the headlights. But I never had enough time to make positive identification.

The birds are hard to see even in daylight. They're brown and black, roughly the color of dead leaves on the forest floor, which not so coincidentally is where they spend their off-duty hours. They even lay their eggs on those leaves, not bothering to build a nest, so sure are they of their camouflage coloring.

So if they didn't whistle, whippoorwills would go almost unnoticed. But then they wouldn't be whippoorwills. These birds, on a soft, warm night, simply can't resist making themselves known.

Any night now, one of the seemingly disembodied voices will come ringing through the darkness.

I'll welcome it—as long as I'm not trying to sleep in a tent.

16

The Art of Sauntering

THE TALL PINES are creaking and groaning in the wind, reminding me of arthritic old men on a cold morning. A big woodpecker is drilling on a dead branch high overhead. White violets are blooming beside the stone wall. I catch a whiff of a familiar fragrance, and in a few minutes find a scraggly lilac bush, hidden in the woods, beside a cellar hole.

I'm learning.

I'm learning the art of sauntering. That's a good word for this lazy-day roaming around, seeing and hearing and trying to notice everything. And it is something of an art, keeping the senses alert. Too often people walk right by interesting things, because they're in a hurry or mired deep in thought or conversation.

As much as I enjoy hiking and "ordinary" walking, I find sauntering can sometimes be more rewarding. Hiking is what I want when exercise is the primary goal, and I'll walk anywhere with an amiable companion, especially an adept conversationalist. But there is also a time to saunter, to wander slowly and freely, unrestricted by time or distance or objectives.

Thoreau was a saunterer. He wrote: "I think I cannot preserve my health and spirits unless I spend four hours a day—and it is commonly more than that—sauntering through the woods and over the hills and fields, absolutely free from worldly engagements."

Few of us get to saunter that often—I know my creditors would object if I loafed four hours a day—but finding a few hours here and there is possible. The trick is to gear down, go slow and easy, and not be concerned about covering ground. Noticing what you pass is more important. For that, sauntering is probably best done alone.

Today I find myself with a rare day off in the middle of the week. That's the best time for sauntering. Not only are the trails and ponds and woods practically deserted now, but there is also something delightful about loafing when you know the rest of the world is working.

I've come out early, to make sure I won't be available if somebody calls, and I've chosen a trail that circles a pond. I've walked it before, but not in spring, and not when I was in the mood to saunter. That makes a difference.

At first I have to remind myself to go slowly: to listen to the trees, to feel the mist rising from the pond. But apparently loafing comes easily to me; in minutes I'm examining sassafras saplings and admiring lichen-covered rocks and trying to identify unseen birds twittering high in the trees.

I come across a garter snake, sunning itself on the rocky trail. Instead of slithering off, as most of its kind would, this one is an aggressive little thing, and repeatedly coils and strikes at my shoe, which I hold a foot or so away. It never touches me, and eventually flips into a trail-side brook and rides the current out of sight.

A chickadee visits me as I walk, traveling along just a few feet away for maybe 50 yards. A wood thrush is singing somewhere in the brush, and jays and crows are loud on the far side of the pond. I notice huge dog tracks on the trail, and raccoon tracks at a mud puddle. A chipmunk pokes its head out of a crevice in a stone wall, then vanishes—far more shy now than in fall, when it would have screamed at me.

About the time I smell the lilac I notice a break in the stone wall and leave the trail to investigate. A dozen yards away is the cellar hole, which I have never noticed before. Not only is the old farm's lilac still persisting, but I also find two gnarled apple trees, remnants or descendants of the vanished farmers' orchard. I wish I had been there when those stubborn old trees were in blossom.

After poking around in the cellar—I find a rusted hoe, minus the handle, and an unbroken milk bottle—I return to the trail. A woodchuck waddles across in front of me. I hear a whir of wings and turn in time to see a grouse fly across a clearing. Doves are calling in the distance.

At the water's edge, I see a turtle climb up onto a rock, to absorb the sunshine. Swallows are soaring above. A mallard flies off. Sunfish are just below the surface, hovering over scooped-out sand areas where they've laid their eggs. A kingfisher perches on a dead pine, strangely silent.

I haven't yet made it halfway around the pond, but already I feel the day is a success. All the things I've seen and heard and felt have been there all along, I'm sure; but because of sauntering, I'm now seeing them. I'm learning.

17

Foreverness of June

THERE IS A FOREVERNESS to June. Wander the countryside now, and it's difficult to picture the time when snow and silence lay upon the land. Autumn and winter must belong to another part of the country; here there is only life and greenery and growth.

This is the way the fields were meant to be, lush with grasses and clover and alfalfa. Haying time. Mow and rake and bale. Then wait a minute, and it will all be tall and thick again.

Right now, that seems possible.

Was there ever a time when that field was barren, frozen rock-hard and buried in snow? No, it couldn't be. Was there a time when the red-winged blackbirds and the meadowlarks did not flush upon our approach, a time when swallows did not swoop low after the mower? It must have been somewhere else. Not here.

Winter can be a shock to the system, no matter how many winters we've been through. It takes some adjustment for the senses to get used to cold wind and snow and bare branches. Autumn, too, even as spectacular as New England autumns are, carries an ominous threat. Leaves fall. Birds depart. They warn us that time is fleeting.

But in June, we are forever young.

Orioles sing as they have every June morning for a thousand years. Daisies bloom in the meadows. Wild roses decorate the fence rows. Bullfrogs ha-rumph in the evening. Fireflies wink in the darkness.

We know this, and expect it. There is no adjustment, no need to get used to an oriole's song. It's there, just as it always was, as it always should be. And, after the second time we hear the oriole, it's difficult to remember there ever was a time when the morning was silent. Realistically, the oriole is only a visitor here—it spends about seven months of each year elsewhere—but nobody can convince me of that right now. Not in June.

April and May are the months when we become reacquainted with the teeming life that vanishes during the winter. And we're surprised every spring when we realize all over again how many mosquitoes and mayflies and nuisance bugs there are. Maybe it's a sign of growing older, but each year there seem to be more of the pesky insects.

Yet, by June, everything falls into place. The mosquitoes are still here, of course, but so are the butterflies. There are more honey bees than hornets around the yard, as many ladybugs as potato beetles in the garden. In June, they belong; they have a place in the scheme of things.

What would a meadow look like without the frosting of daisies? I can't remember. When we walk there now we talk about the year our daughters picked bouquets of daisies for Father's Day, and how the daisies never seem to have a bad year, and how they just get taller if the grass and weeds are allowed to grow tall. Daisies are June. Dependable. Forever.

We pick the first wild fruits of the year, the sweet strawberries of some sunny hillside, and we can literally taste summer. Can it really be

a year since the last time we ate wild strawberries off the vine? No, that can't be. Maybe it was last week, but not last year!

We know that raspberries are ripening now, that blackberries and blueberries and elderberries are to follow in rapid succession. It happens every summer; there is no change to the order.

The streams and brooks run clear and cool. As always. They may dry up next month, ice over in winter and overflow with raging floods in early spring, but now the brooks are the way we remember them. Sparkling and gurgling. A kingfisher above and a frog at the shore and a dragonfly hovering over the water. Right now, I can't picture a brook in snow.

Somewhere, in the dim recesses of memory, I recall a stormy night last winter when we sat before the fireplace and talked of summer. We talked of how that night, with its snow and wind and frigid temperatures, was the price we paid for June. We talked of the brooks and the strawberries, of the daisies and the orioles. It was easy; they are so deeply imprinted on the mind.

Yet, it is much more difficult now to think of the opposite side of the circle. Snow? What's that? A tree without leaves? A woods without birdsong? Do those things really happen?

Try it sometime. Walk in the dewy morning. Listen to the orioles. Smell the freshly mowed hay. Pluck a handful of daisies. And just try to think of what the other seasons are like. Try to remember what it is like without all the riches of summer.

It's not easy. Not now. Not in June.

18

Rainbow Magic

RAINBOWS ARE MAGIC. That's what I thought as a small child and that's what I believe today. Yes, I know that science can explain rainbows, but each time I see those glorious stripes of colors arching across the sky, I still think of magic. Scientific explanations seem woefully inadequate.

> *Rainbow: A bow or arc of prismatic colors appearing in the heavens opposite the sun and caused by the refraction and reflection of the sun's rays in drops of rain.*

That's one dictionary's definition. I don't think it even comes close to doing justice to rainbows. Seven ribbons of distinct colors appear in the sky, stretching for miles from horizon to horizon. Sometimes, the seven stripes are even repeated, in reverse order, making a double rainbow. That's more than a mere natural happenstance; that's magic.

As a kid, I used to fantasize about what it would be like to fly into a rainbow. I imagined slicing into the aura of red light, and then moving on to the orange and yellow and other colors. I wondered how long it would take to pass through each phase, how wide those bands actually were. Would they be "fuzzy," like a colored cloud, or would they be clear, something like red or blue sunshine? Would a rainbow look as lovely from the inside as it did from the ground?

Obviously, nobody can see a rainbow from the inside. Even I have to accept that. The proper distance is required to see the colors —proper distance and proper position in relation to the sun, and the proper angle of sunshine hitting the falling rain.

By the way, scientists say that for double rainbows to occur, the drops of water even have to be of proper size and shape. I'll let scientists worry about such things. I'll just enjoy the show.

Certain rainbows stand out in memory.

There were 14 of us in the group, 14 wet and cold and hungry and miserable canoeists. We had been caught in a heavy shower while crossing a large pond in Maine, and now we were trying to get a campfire going, so that we could warm up and start drying our gear.

Then the sun broke through, low in the west, and a masterpiece of a rainbow popped out. I remember somebody shouting, "Look at that!" and somebody else murmured a soft "Wow!" and "Fantastic!," but mostly we stared at it in silent awe. We were still wet and hungry, but suddenly our spirits lifted. That evening became the most memorable of the 10-day trip.

Other rainbows come to mind, too. Years ago, one so impressed our daughter that she alerted all the neighbors, most of whom joined us in the street. I remember another that appeared over flat farmlands in the Midwest and seemed to be radiating from the church steeples in two villages. And perhaps our son might recall one that disrupted a Little League game he was playing in, because all the boys were watching the sky.

But, in a way, every rainbow is special.

I'm not sure I'll ever be able to comprehend the fact that all of that color, all that beauty, is created from thin air and moving raindrops and sunshine. No matter what science says, there has to be magic at work in this. There has to be.

19

Teach-er, Teach-er

W<small>E HADN'T GONE</small> 500 feet. We hadn't been walking ten minutes. And we had already found the bird that was to be the object of our day's search. That happens sometimes.

But it wasn't all luck. I was smart enough to take an expert along, somebody who can pick out individual sounds amid the din of bird song that can envelop a favored woodland on a sparkling spring morning. Without my companion, I might have walked all day without finding this bird. It's tough when you have a tin ear.

We were looking for an ovenbird, a brownish little ground bird that I find intriguing because of its name, which comes from the nest it builds. That nest, made of leaves, grasses and plant fibers, is placed on the ground, then covered with a unique domed roof. The result is something resembling an old Dutch oven—truly a work of art.

Finding the nest was too much to ask—that requires hours and hours of patient observation or an exorbitant amount of dumb luck. I was willing to settle for just seeing the bird up close. But to my companion, that was no challenge at all. Ovenbird songs are loud and distinctive, I was told. We would be hearing them all morning; the birds would be easy to find. For an expert, perhaps. But not for me. It's tough when you have a tin ear.

Even after roaming around the woods and fields for years, I can identify very few birds by their voices alone. The mourning dove and the quail, the chickadee and the blue jay, sometimes a cardinal, maybe a song sparrow. They are birds I've known all my life; even somebody with a tin ear has to learn something.

All of the above are birds that spend the entire year here. Migrants cause me a lot more trouble. I recognize red-winged blackbirds and kingfishers by their calls each spring, but when other birds return and start singing, I have to try learning what is what all over again each year. I seldom even know the robin's tune, or the oriole's, or the yellowthroat's, the first time I hear it. By the time I no longer have to ask, "What bird is that?," it's time for them to stop singing for the year.

So I looked for help when I wanted to find the ovenbird. It's considered a large warbler, but I think of it as a small thrush. It has the olive-brown back of the thrushes, plus a streaked "necklace" across the chest, similar to the underside markings on some thrushes. What sets it apart from thrushes is a bright-orange crown, a stripe across the head. Of course, you have to be close to the bird to see that stripe, and since the bird is heard far more than seen, I turned to the expert.

We chose this particular woods not merely because it was likely to have ovenbirds—most woods do, I was informed—but also because my companion considered it a potential spot for scarlet tanagers. Experts have favorite birds, too. Tanagers are truly spectacular birds, blood red except for the wings, which are jet black. We've gone looking for them before and made something of a game of it, seeing if I could find one simply by spotting its brilliant colors in the treetops before the expert

could find one by its song. I seldom win such games.

Before heading out that morning, I tried to prepare myself. No point in looking worse than necessary. One guidebook said: "Once it has become familiar, the voice of the ovenbird is one of the most obvious in the woods. The song begins softly and builds to a ringing crescendo—teacher, teacher, teacher!" Another description was similar: "Its song is an emphatic teach'er, teach'er, TEACH'ER, repeated rapidly in crescendo. In some areas, monosyllabic, with little change in emphasis, TEACH, TEACH, TEACH."

Still another book said that the monosyllabic ovenbirds are those below the Mason-Dixon line. I never knew before that birds develop regional accents. Hmmmm. Would that mean that New England ovenbirds say teach'ah?

Anyway, we had barely started down a gravel lane in the woods when my companion stopped me. "Listen, there's your ovenbird. That didn't take too long, did it?" I listened and heard a long and loud song coming from the brush. It didn't sound like teach'er to me, or even teach'ah, but it was cheery and pleasant. In a minute, my expert located the bird for me. It was perched on a low branch, its head thrown back, pouring out its heart and soul in song.

We walked for a couple of hours, and heard and saw the bird so often that even I had my fill of ovenbirds. We also found two tanagers—I lost the game both times—and dozens of other birds. Many of the singers remained invisible, and I had to take my guide's word for most of the sounds: "That's a parula warbler." "Hear that prairie warbler?" "That sounds like a white-eyed vireo."

Still, I was gaining some confidence, and as we neared the car and the end of our walk, I beat the expert to the punch on what sounded to me like a loud, emphatic crescendo. Nice of our ovenbird to say good-bye, I said as casually as I could. My companion looked at me a moment, then said rather sadly, "That wasn't an ovenbird. That was a towhee. It says its name."

Yes, birding is tough when you have a tin ear.

20

Thunderstorms

LIGHTNING SEEMS TO RIP the blackened sky apart. The jagged bolts, crackling downward from boiling clouds, are almost blinding in their brilliance. Booming thunder follows: immense crashing explosions that make the huge trees tremble and the ground shudder. Then comes a pelting, drenching rain.

Ah, a summer thunderstorm. Isn't it beautiful?

I know not everybody agrees, but thunderstorms can be fascinating. I like all storms—blizzards, sleet, nor'easters, even hurricanes—anything that shows the might of wind and waves, ice and snow. But there is something special about summer thunderstorms. Lightning and thunder are awesome. It's hard to imagine something so bright, so loud—so violent—being created by something so flimsy as air and clouds.

Sometimes, the storm can be a blessing, a way of breaking a heat wave or drought. And sometimes, you can sense it coming.

All day the air has been still and heavy, the heat oppressive. It's the type of day that makes me glad somebody invented air conditioning. And fans. And ice cubes.

Insects are droning, but it's too hot for the birds. They are silent, sulking in the shade, beaks agape. Even the leaves are feeling the heat, hanging limp from the branches. It's as if the entire world were suffering, awaiting relief.

By evening, a bank of clouds has appeared in the west. Then more clouds—clouds piled on top of clouds. They're not black, but neither are they the white, cottony clouds that have floated across the sky day after day during this drought. These seem thicker, more ominous.

Then, just about the time some of the clouds turn inside out—revealing darker, angrier colors—a rush of cooler air sweeps across the land. It's a sweet breeze, the kind that billows curtains at open windows. It's the kind of breeze that used to make me go out and run with the wind at my back when I was a kid. It was like flying. Loved that feeling.

A low rumble then starts in the distance. Often, the sky above is still blue and the sunshine still bright. I have to listen carefully to make sure it's not some traffic or a plane.

But then, as the darker clouds appear and move closer, the first flashes of lightning can be seen. At first, there is a momentary lapse between the lightning and the thunder. But the time span quickly shrinks. Soon the flashes and the crashes are almost simultaneous.

The storm is here.

Rain starts with big, splattering drops. They raise tiny clouds of dust in the fields and splash audibly on roofs and rocks and sidewalks. In seconds, the individual drops are smaller, but now there are millions of them: a torrent. No more dust. The force of the rain batters the leaves and plants, but even as they are being beaten down each one seems to reach upward, as if welcoming the life-giving nourishment.

Whether the storm lasts only a minute or an hour, once it is over it is time to go out and marvel. The air is fresh and cool, the countryside scrubbed and shiny. What had been a parched, stagnant land is now vibrant, renewed. After such a storm, it seems that I can see the flowers and leaves and grass growing.

My favorite thunderstorms are those that arrive late at night. When lightning and thunder rock me from a deep sleep, they take on an eerie quality. Unlike daytime storms, those of the night seem to explode without warning from the darkness—larger, more menacing but also more magnificent than during the day. Nothing sets off the startling brightness and colors of lightning like the black background of night.

I have no idea how many hours I've spent at windows watching midnight storms. Each time, I stay until the lightning starts to fade, until the fury subsides. And each time, I am left strangely, perhaps smugly, contented. The world has just been revitalized in spectacular fashion, and I am the privileged witness.

21

Friendly Enemies

DISCRETION MAY BE the better part of valor after all. Even for a woodchuck. Either that, or the old 'chuck decided that after barely avoiding the jaws of a big red dog for several years, the odds were mounting against him.

Whatever the reason, the woodchuck that used to live in the field beyond my backyard has moved out. I'm not sure that's good news. What is Rusty going to stalk and chase this summer? He's too slow for rabbits, and squirrels cheat by climbing trees. That woodchuck was his chance to pretend he was a hunter.

They were something to watch, an aging dog and a roly-poly woodchuck that must have been past middle age himself. They appeared to be playing a game, but it was a deadly game—or would have been if Rusty had ever won. He has dispatched numerous other woodchucks over the years, but this one was always a little too quick, or a little too smart.

Maybe that's why the woodchuck moved away. Maybe he was smart enough to realize that woodchucks age even faster than dogs, that his speed would fail sooner or later. He had phenomenal timing; invariably, his last leap into his burrow left Rusty snapping at thin air, perhaps two inches behind. The woodchuck knew exactly how far he could wander from that tunnel, exactly when to start his retreat.

I think Rusty enjoyed the game, even though he came out second best every time. Every few weeks during the summer, he would pick an evening and lie out in the backyard, carefully studying the weedy meadow beyond. When the woodchuck emerged from his den, on the far side of the field, Rusty's ears would perk up, and his body would tremble slightly.

For a few moments, he would watch from
the yard as the woodchuck sat up and
looked around. It wasn't until the
'chuck started feeding, chew-
ing up clover and grasses and
other plants, that Rusty would
start making his move.

First, he would slink
slowly along the low stone
wall beside the garden. If he
reached the meadow unde-
tected, he would pause
awhile beside the raspberry
tangle, then inch forward, a
step at a time. Sometimes, he
would even drop down and crawl, trying to stay hidden.

There was no doubt the woodchuck knew exactly where Rusty was
all the time. He would go on eating, frequently glancing around to gauge
Rusty's progress, but he never seemed to worry, and never ventured far
from home. When the dog got uncomfortably close, the 'chuck would
edge ever so slightly back toward his burrow; when Rusty made his rush,
the 'chuck would scramble toward the tunnel. It was a close race every
time, and the 'chuck won every time. I think Rusty once got a mouthful
of hair from the woodchuck's tail, but that was as close as he came during
the times I watched.

When the skirmishes first
began, Rusty wouldn't give up
easily. He'd bark and
growl and try dig-
ging into the
den. But over
the last two
summers, Rusty
changed his atti-
tude. Once the
w o o d c h u c k
vanished into
his hole, Rusty

would simply sniff around a moment and then trot back to the yard. No barking, no growling. Not even a backward glance. Nor did he ever wait around the yard to see if the woodchuck would come out again. One run a night was enough. It was almost as if actually catching the critter was no longer that important. It's not whether you win or lose, you know; it's how you play the game.

Of course, Rusty has managed to rationalize most of his failings. Once he loved chasing rabbits, but even when he was young he couldn't catch them. Now, when we happen to flush one while out walking, he quickly looks the other way and pretends he hasn't seen it. Less embarrassing that way.

He was our squirrel warden, too, taking it upon himself to protect the bird feeder from squirrels that stole sunflower seeds. Eventually, though, he decided it wasn't fair for squirrels to simply sit up in trees while he barked frantically below. So these days he chases squirrels only when we're in the yard with him, and he has to put on a good show. Squirrels are no fun.

Now his woodchuck, the only wild animal that gave him a sporting chance, has moved away. I think he misses him already.

A few days ago, I found a new woodchuck den, perhaps a quarter-mile away on the bank of a small stream. I have no idea if it's the same 'chuck, but I like to think it is. It's the kind of place a smart old 'chuck would choose, a good retirement home.

I have a decision to make. Should I let the woodchuck live out its days in peace? Or should I take Rusty down there and see if he can make one last catch? He probably can't, but it seems he should have one final try. I'm still not sure which way to go.

22

Morning on the Mountain

RIGHT ON CUE, the overcast dissolved—just melted away. As we stepped beyond the tree line, sunshine that had been AWOL all morning flowed down and lit up the forested valleys and ridges spread out below us. The remaining clouds swirled around higher peaks to our north for a few minutes, then gradually drifted away.

We dropped our packs and sat on the rocks, all the sweaty struggle of the previous hours falling away as easily as the weight of the packs. This was our objective: to sit up there, amid a carpet of alpine flowers, the majesty of the mountains all around us—and have the place to ourselves.

We were on Mount Pierce, a 4,300-foot knob near the southern end of New Hampshire's Presidential Range, and during our stay on the summit we owned that magnificent view. Below were the ravines that lead to Crawford Notch. In front of us were the imposing peaks of Mount Eisenhower, Mount Franklin, Mount Monroe and the big one itself, Mount Washington.

On our way up, we had passed two young men who were heading down after spending the night at an Appalachian Mountain Club hut. Later, we saw a couple on the trail to Eisenhower, a considerable distance ahead of us. Other than that, the four of us felt the mountain was ours.

This was to be an experiment. We wanted to test the often-heard criticism that the mountains are too crowded these days; that there no longer is such a thing as solitude on the high peaks of the White Mountains.

I've seen some of that congestion on the better-known trails of

Mount Washington. Once, about halfway up Tuckerman Ravine, I sat on a rock for a half-hour and counted the hikers streaming by. The number was 24. I haven't been on that trail since.

So we looked for somewhere else to walk. We wanted a trail that would provide the views and that was also not so obscure or so strenuous that it wouldn't be a true test of crowds. There are dozens of trails that are never crowded because few people know about them, or they are so difficult that they seem designed by mountain goats.

We wanted a trail that would get us above the tree line in a relatively short time; whose beginning was easily accessible; and one that most mountain hikers had at least heard of. A friend who has hiked all over the White Mountains suggested the Crawford Path. Great choice.

It has everything we sought.

It's well known. A sign at the start, on Route 302 north of Bartlett, claims it is the "oldest continually hiked trail in America." I doubt that it has actually been continually hiked since first established, by Abel

Crawford in 1819, but there was a time when taking Crawford Path all the way to Mount Washington was the thing to do. For a while, it was even used as a bridle path, but there have been no horses up there for years (and in some of the steep areas I think I'd rather trust my own footing over a horse's).

It's short. From the start to the summit of Pierce—which some people still call by its old name, Mount Clinton—is approximately three miles. We came down by way of the AMC's Mizpah Spring Hut, adding perhaps a half-mile to the six-mile round trip.

Although steep in places, the trail has been graded; that is, rocks have been repositioned to make climbing less difficult. Also, there are many bridges over brooks and wet ground.

It's wild. Almost from the start, we were pausing to check out the flowers. In the lower woods were red trilliums and trout lilies and bunchberries and lots of lady's-slippers, including one that was pure white. Up higher we passed less familiar plants, like white trilliums and others that made us wish we had brought along an alpine-flower guide. Later, at Mizpah Hut, we looked up some of the plants in books and discovered that we had seen rhodora and mountain heath and Labrador tea. We learned the tiny flowers that covered the wind-swept summit itself—the ones that reminded me of wild-strawberry blossoms—are called diapensias. I probably won't remember the name, but I'll remember the scene.

Red squirrels were all around us. Unseen thrushes sang back in the woods. At one point, a grouse rocketed out of a thicket just a few steps off the trail.

It's picturesque. Long before we reached the overlooks, there were places to linger. At its start, the trail follows a tumbling stream, named Gibbs Brook, and short side trails lead to several waterfalls. By New Hampshire standards, the falls are not spectacular, but to people used to walking in Rhode Island, they are worth a pause.

Best of all, though, on that day the trail had solitude. Later I realized we were a little early in the year for our trip to be an accurate test. It was early June, only the beginning of hiking time in the mountains. Schools were not yet out.

But if there is a secret to avoiding crowds on mountain trails, other than going in the off-seasons, it might be this: Start out early in the day. We didn't get going on Mount Pierce until about 8 a.m., but in July and August I would shoot for as early as 5 or 5:30. In addition to avoiding the crowds this way, there is no better time to be outdoors than the first few hours after daybreak; and if you are making a strenuous climb in summer, the coolness of morning is priceless.

There are plenty of times for sleeping in or dallying over breakfast—but not when the mountains await. Not for me. I want to linger along a trail and not worry about others walking up my back. I want uninterrupted moments to contemplate rock-ribbed peaks that poke into the clouds. I want to sit on a summit and hear only the wind. That means beating the crowds. It's well worth missing a couple of hours of sleep.

23

Raspberries

THE TIME HAS COME. I've always liked raspberries, but enough is enough. I have to start cutting them back before they take over the place. Right after I pick this year's fruit.

Raspberries—the wild, black-capped kind—have been a part of my summers as long as I can remember. As a kid, I tagged along with Mom when she went picking berries in Gib's Woods. While she worked, I roamed around. Those trips were my introduction to squirrels and catbirds and sassafras leaves and day lilies.

And I developed a strong liking for those berries. They are smaller and seedier than domestic raspberries, to be sure, but I find them juicier and sweeter.

We practically lived on raspberries in those days, but we never got tired of them. In fact, I recently discovered that my brothers and sisters still go searching for raspberries each summer, even though many of them now live in cities. They find the berries in vacant lots and along railroad tracks and on river banks. I guess we all remember Gib's Woods.

When I moved to New England, I was pleasantly surprised to find a great many raspberries growing in sprawling brambles near my new home. I'm not sure just why I was so surprised—probably because New England is known much more for blueberries than raspberries—but I soon found I could pick all I wanted without going a hundred yards from my house.

At that time, the bushes were scattered about. The largest concentration was on a knoll I soon named Raspberry Hill. There were also brambles in a meadow beyond the backyard, several bushes along a path that ran through the woods, and a couple of bushes that had recently sprouted in a weedy, rock-strewn corner of the lot where I eventually decided to make a garden.

I developed a regular picking route. I usually hit Raspberry Hill first, because picking was easiest there. Then I'd move on to the meadow and the woods path before finishing up with the bushes nearest the house. I collected berries by the gallons. I collected plenty of scratches and mosquito bites, too, and once in a while I ran into hornets. But by mid-July we had enough raspberries in the freezer to keep us in pies and jellies through the following winter.

Time changes everything, though. A bulldozer flattened Raspberry Hill and houses now stand where I used to fill my buckets. Trees along the woods' path grew taller and thicker, and gradually allowed too little sunshine to reach the berry bushes. Those bushes produced fewer berries each year, and soon may die out altogether. Brambles in the meadow flourished for a while, but apparently became victims of their own growth. As the bushes became larger and older, they produced less fruit. I recall that happened in Gib's Woods, too. Raspberries grow on new canes; too much "old wood" inhibits production.

Still, there was no need for concern. I was picking berries galore from the bushes near my garden. Those bushes had lots of sunshine and received enough water and fertilizer, in accidental doses, from the garden to keep them thriving. And each spring I whacked off some of the vines —not because it would promote heavier production, but because the canes kept trying to steal some of my garden space.

It was a constant battle, and now it appears I'm losing. This spring, I noticed the raspberries had claimed far more ground than I had realized. They've not only crept out several feet on the east side, where they've always been, but now they've somehow jumped across to the north side and are invading a section that had been reserved for other fruit. Raspberry vines are mixing in with the grapes and currants and gooseberries, and some appear to be trying to climb into the young peach and plum trees.

Enough is enough. I like raspberries, but I cannot let them take over the entire yard. I've got to get ruthless. No more mere trimming back the outer vines. I have to get right to the heart of the matter, chopping out the parent canes in the middle of the bushes. Even that won't eradicate them, because they'll start coming right back next spring. Once a raspberry vine has taken hold, it's not going to yield very easily.

Of course, I cannot cut them all back at the same time. If I did, it would be a few years before they are nuisances again, but it also would be a few years before I'd get berries again. And I'm not sure I can go through a July without picking raspberries. That would be against family tradition.

I'll do a few each year, starting with the bushes that are threatening my peach and plum trees. They should never have been allowed to sprout there. They definitely have to go. Right after I'm finished with the picking.

24

The Fiddlers

THE BEACH SCENE never changes much, does it? Males sprawl all over the sand, soaking up the sun, until a pretty female passes by. Then each one snaps to attention and flexes his muscles, doing his best to get the lady to notice him.

Just so he can fiddle around.

It happens every summer. In fact, almost every day during the summer.

I'm referring to fiddler crabs, of course. What other kind of males would act like that?

Fiddler crabs are intriguing little creatures of the shorelines and weedy coves. They're called fiddlers because the males have one unusually large claw that, to the imaginative, resembles a fiddle. It's so out of proportion—at least 20 times larger than the other claw—that it must be a bass fiddle.

They're "on" most of the time, but when I watch the crabs I think of them as conductors, rather than performers. Each male spends a lot of time waving that huge claw as if directing some invisible orchestra in some inaudible symphony. Only he can see the players and only he can hear the music, but that doesn't matter. He swings that massive baton back and forth, on and on. Nothing else is as important. Not even eating.

Naturalists, of course, have a more fundamental explanation for the crab's waving. It's courtship, and maybe finding the right mate—or any mate—really is more important than eating. The males can't sing, like birds, or croak, like frogs—they don't even have strings on their fiddles to strum—so they have to get their female friends to take notice some other way. They wave: Hey, over here! How about me?

It can be a chaotic method. Perhaps not quite as bizarre as the spring peepers' frantic din in April, but almost. It's always bewildered me how peepers—tiny tree frogs—can choose prospective mates from the hundreds that are trilling simultaneously in each small pond. The crabs' waving looks almost as confusing, since it's supposed to be both a come-hither lure for the females and a this-is-my-turf warning to other males.

Like the peepers, the fiddlers live in colonies, so close together their burrows in the sand may be only inches apart. That leads to some spirited competition for the ladies. And some sneaky winners.

Not long ago, I saw a female crab (the females' two claws are of equal size, so the sexes are easy to distinguish) approach an area where numerous males were posed at their burrow entrances, hypnotically waving their fiddles. This damsel was not mesmerized, however, and as the nearest male tried to coax her into his pad she resisted, pausing a few moments and then slowly circling away. Just flirting, it looked to me. Playing hard to get.

Her detour took her into another male's territory, and that fiddler rushed out to make his pitch for the female. He and the first suitor then locked claws, but there wasn't much of a battle. They sort of waltzed around, pushing each other, without landing any damaging blows. It reminded me of a hockey fight.

Meanwhile, the female wandered toward a third male, who immediately recognized an opportunity when he saw one. He darted between the brawlers and the female, and deftly maneuvered her into his own burrow; then he disappeared into the tunnel after her, leaving the other males to tussle and wonder what happened. I imagine there was a good bit of gloating going on down in that burrow.

More often when a female seems interested, the male ducks into the burrow first, expecting her to follow. But she doesn't always do as expected. I watched one female saunter through an area that must have had 50 males coming on to her. Large males and small ones. Those with yellow claws, those with gray claws. Some had whitish shells, some black, and quite a lot had colorful purple-and-ivory patterned backs that resembled marble.

This gal was picky. I counted eight times that she expressed interest in a male, followed him to a burrow entrance, looked inside, but then moved on. Maybe she was looking for shag carpeting, or a fancy stereo, or crystal chandeliers. Who knows? Whatever it was, the ninth tunnel had it, and she disappeared inside behind a mid-sized male with a pale-yellow fiddle. I'd love to know what he had that the others didn't.

Apparently, females can afford to be picky. For every female, there seem to be dozens of males. And while the males customarily hang around their burrows, the females are always on the move, usually in a hurry—they have the chance of meeting lots of males. Of course, with that many males seeking, uh, companionship, I suppose the females have to keep moving.

Beach scenes are all alike, aren't they?

Summer

25

Haying

HAYING IS SO much easier now. I don't mind it at all anymore. Making hay is work. It's hot, dirty, itchy work. But I look forward to haying time now. Mainly because somebody else does it.

Haying season is one of those times when I have to drive down from the hills and out of the woods—I have to go to the farms and fields. I have to smell again the fresh-cut hay. It's an aroma that is sweeter to me than the fragrance of any flower.

I don't know if those who've never farmed, or lived in farming areas, have the same feeling, but to me, new hay is the essence of summer. That smell always takes me back to a time and place I cherish. Maybe an old sailor who has been away from the sea for a while and then gets a whiff of salt air can understand.

But I haven't forgotten all the other aspects of haying. Especially the way I did it. My family made hay the old-fashioned way—by hand. Well, semi- old-fashioned: we didn't cut or rake it by hand, but we sometimes forked it onto a wagon by hand, and always had to fork it up into the barn lofts by hand. Those who use balers and conveyor belts don't realize how much better they have it.

I'd still be willing to do the early stages of haying—mowing and raking were downright pleasant (particularly if it meant staying home from school for the day).

The tractor was noisy and the mower clattered, but when I was out there on a sunny morning, with nobody else around, the hayfield was an enchanting place. The clover and alfalfa and timothy, damp with dew, glistened; meadowlarks and red-winged blackbirds sang, or scolded me

for invading their domain; barn swallows followed the mower, swooping down on the insects it uncovered.

Occasionally a rabbit or quail was flushed; when I could, I would stop and lift the blade over the baby rabbits or quail eggs. Pheasants often stayed on their nests, unnoticed until too late. Destroying an animal took a good chunk of the enjoyment out of mowing.

If the day was hot, the curing started quickly, and so I could luxuriate in the hay smell. Raking was next, which was fun, but I seldom got to do it, because I didn't drive straight enough for Dad; he liked perfect windrows.

My uncle Gib would often bring over his buckrake to scoop up the hay and haul it home. The contraption was an ancient truck with long, pointed forklike poles hooked on behind. He backed into the windrow until he had a load, then lifted it a few feet with a motorized winch, and drove to the barn. There he would dump it on the dirt floor and head out for another load.

That's when haying ceased to be pleasant. We'd take pitchforks and toss the hay into the loft, all the dirt and chaff drifting back down on top of us. Once up in the loft the older boys distributed the hay while the younger kids trudged back and forth, compacting the hay to make room for more.

It became a point of pride to get the entire load forked into the loft and scattered before Gib got back with the next load. That was easy at first, but as the day wore on, things got tougher. Not only did the piles in the loft get higher, but the heat inside the barn increased dramatically. Especially up there under the eaves, beneath the tin roof. Right where I always seemed to wind up. Between loads I'd climb to the "pigeon hole" at the roof's apex to get a breath of air.

When we finished our own haying, Dad would let us hire out to other farmers. Working for other people was almost easy. Not only did we get paid, but everybody else seemed to have balers. All we had to do was take the bales as the machine spat them out and stack them on the wagon; then, at the barn, put them on an elevator that took them into the loft, and there stack them. Still plenty of sweaty work, though nothing like handling loose hay.

But now it's nice to just drive out to the farms, let the aromas drift over me . . . and watch somebody else do all the work.

26

The Performer

I WONDER IF OUR snake will be back this year. It made working in the garden quite an experience last summer.

It was an eastern hognosed snake, sometimes called a puff adder. Anyone who has ever come in contact with a hognose knows why it is interesting. It's a performer.

Hognosed snakes are harmless. They never bite, but they certainly pretend to be fierce. They coil their tails, lift their heads as if to strike, hiss menacingly, and spread their neck muscles cobra-style. They look for all the world like a deadly viper to be given a wide berth.

If that doesn't work, they play dead.

When they realize that their ruse is not scaring you away, they'll suddenly go into a death scene that would put even the best opossum to shame. They'll roll over on their backs, open their mouths, let their tongues hang out, squirm about in death throes for a few seconds, then lie still. Belly up. As dead as last week's baseball scores.

It's something to see.

Right here, let me say that I'm not a snake person. I can appreciate most things in the woods and fields and swamps, but snakes leave me cold. Toads and hornets are okay, in their places. So are vultures and mice and lizards. I'll even go looking for snapping turtles and some kinds of caterpillars.

But snakes? No thanks.

Even though I know there are no really dangerous snakes here, and I know they can be valuable for keeping down the populations of mice and other pests, the first snake I come upon each spring, even if it's only a pencil-thin garter snake, still sends that shiver of terror through me. It's a built-in reflex, I suppose, and I keep trying to overcome it, but so far there has been little progress.

Maybe it goes back to that time when I was a little kid and, on a dare, I grabbed a snake that was sunning itself on a pile of rocks. Both its head and tail were under rocks, and it turned out to be much larger—MUCH larger—than I expected. By the time I had pulled the entire thing out, I had about five feet of writhing snake in my hands.

Now I'm pretty cautious about what I pick up.

I had seen a hognosed snake in action before ours arrived last summer, so I recognized the short, thick body and blunted "nose" and called the kids around to watch the show. Right on cue, it reared up defiantly, hissed at me and made several quick lunges. It was so convincing I began wondering if I really knew what I was talking about, after all.

It didn't seem in a hurry to play dead, so I reached out to it with a stick—some people use their hands, but not me—and patted it on the back. Just like that, it "died," gasping out a final breath as it wriggled its last.

We stepped back and waited. In a minute or two, the tongue slipped back inside the mouth. Then it moved its head just enough to take a peek at us, to see if we were still there. When I took one step toward it, it went back into its trance. I reached down and rolled it onto its belly, and immediately it flipped over onto its back once more.

It remained that way until we retreated from the garden. Then, very slowly, it came back to life and eventually slithered out of sight into a raspberry bramble.

A day or two later, the snake was back, and we saw it occasionally for about ten days, usually in the late afternoon. It might have become a permanent resident had it not been for two side effects of his presence.

The first was that hognosed snakes love to eat toads—some live almost exclusively on toads—and we like having toads around the garden because they devour so many insects. We decided our garden needed something that took care of the aphids and mites and grubs more than we needed a showman.

The other reason we sent the snake packing was that, no matter how "cute" it was, few members of the family were willing to dash out to the garden for a tomato or a couple of carrots. One suddenly becomes a little reluctant to reach down into thick vines and greenery, knowing a good-sized snake might be resting down there.

So the day came when, during its death act, I picked up the snake—for me, that took willpower—and carried it across the meadow beyond the backyard. There I released it, among a jumble of rocks and logs and brush. It appeared to be a good spot for toads and other snake goodies, and I hope the hognose found happiness.

Now it's summer again and the garden is filling up with vines and leaves. I saw a toad out there the other day, and it reminded me of the snake.

I would not mind at all if it came back. For one performance.

27

Summer in the Orchard

Midsummer approaches and we look for escapes. To beaches. To mountains. For a day. For a week. Just get away. Find someplace a little cooler.

Sometimes it's worth the effort; sometimes not. It certainly would be easier, and it might be just as comfortable, retreating to the apple orchard.

That's what my brothers and I did as kids. When hot weather came, and we had finished the first rounds of haying and hoeing, we spent a lot of hours in the apple trees. Just goofing off.

We'd climb into the trees, sometimes constructing rude platforms we called treehouses, sometimes examining bird nests, sometimes just seeing how high we could climb. A little later in the summer, we'd test-taste the green apples, lying to each other about how great they were. Mostly, though, we just sat in the cool trees and talked.

Of course, our orchard was not like the commercial orchards around these days. Now, all the trees are identical, kept small for easy picking, pruned into grotesque shapes, sprayed so heavily that not a butterfly or ladybug would dare venture into those branches, much less a bluebird or oriole.

We grew all kinds of apples, but each tree was an individual. I loved the names my father used for the trees—Northern Spy, Ben Davis, Grimes Golden, Gravenstein, Sheepnose, Jonathan, Baldwin, Winesap —but eventually we gave most of the trees more personal names like Old Car Tree and Umbrella Tree and Pig Puddle Tree and Third Base Tree. We had early apples and late apples. Red apples and yellow apples.

Eating apples and cooking apples.
Even one magical tree that bore
five different varieties.

Each tree grew in its own
shape, to its own size. Some
became giants, far too
tall for our ladders,
but I don't recall
any of them
b e i n g
t r i m m e d
back. I'm
sure pruning
would have in-
creased the pro-
duction, but that
was something we
never worried about.
We always had far more
apples than we could use.

You see, we weren't in
the apple business; these dozens and dozens of trees were only
for my own family. And even a
family of that size—seven boys and
six girls—could never eat that many
apples.

All the surrounding farms also
had their own orchards—self-sufficiency was a point of pride in those
days—but few could match ours. My great-grandmother had planted the
trees decades earlier, and I always thought she had gotten a little carried
away. But there was a time, when my parents moved onto the farm during
the Depression, that the orchard played a major role in putting food on
the table. That was a little before my time, but I've heard they gathered
up apples by the barrels and filled the cellar with them. Mom says she
dreamed up new recipes that featured apples every week.

Later, many of the less-appealing apples were wasted. Sometimes,
after a summer windstorm, the ground would be littered with green

apples, so many that we kids would have to rake them together and carry them off in baskets to prevent our cows, which were penned in the orchard at night, from eating too many and getting sick. Of course, first we dallied a few hours building Apple Town, outlining dozens of streets and buildings with the useless fruit. And it wasn't unusual for us to get into an apple war, firing the hard little apples at each other. I never enjoyed that much. Those apples hurt, and I couldn't throw them straight enough to hit anybody else.

Our favorite trees for climbing were a Northern Spy and one we called the Yellow Apple Tree—I never did learn its real name. The Northern Spy leaned at such an angle we could literally run up the trunk. At least a few feet. One of our games was seeing who could go highest without touching the tree with his hands. The Yellow Apple was simply an easy tree to climb, had thick, comfortable branches for sitting on, and had the earliest ripening apples in the entire orchard. But as I remember it, we seldom allowed those apples to turn yellow; most were eaten while still green.

Harder to climb but producing the best apples was a slender Sheepnose that grew in an open area at the center of the orchard. It had only a few apples each year for some reason, but they were superb. We watched that tree closely, and when we noticed a particularly divine apple starting to ripen, one of us would "claim" it. That meant the rest of us were honor-bound not to touch it. So strong was this code of ethics we wouldn't pick a claimed apple even if Mom sent us out there for materials for a pie or dumplings or cobbler.

Often, those special apples were high in the tree, far out of reach—the excuse we always gave Mom if she asked—but when it came time for the lucky kid to collect his prize we had ways. Usually, we threw other apples or short sticks at the branch holding the apple. We became so adept at this we could—most of the time—clip off the apple without touching it. One of us would then catch it before it hit the ground. No bruises. The "owner" then would shine it up and eat it as slowly as he could, particularly if others were around to watch in envy.

Only once can I remember claiming a Sheepnose that actually made it to maturity unmarred. Sometimes, they were pecked by birds; sometimes they fell before ripening; sometimes they were knocked down by an errant softball—the tree was just beyond shortstop. But one time my Sheepnose turned out perfect, red and shiny, with the peculiar oblong shape that gives the variety its name. My brothers kept telling me it was full of worms, but I knew they would trade any of their apples for it.

When the day came that it looked ready, three brothers went along for the ceremonial feast. They even volunteered to bring it down for me, but this was my apple; I wanted to do it all myself. My first three throws hit wrong branches, knocking down several other apples and a great many leaves. Then, I picked up a rock and fired once more. It struck the apple dead-center. Smash! Instant applesauce. I thought my brothers would never stop laughing.

28

Reward of the Hummingbird

MOM WAS RIGHT, after all. She used to insist that "no good deed ever goes unrewarded." But I'm not sure she was talking about hummingbirds as our reward.

Hummingbirds are among our favorite birds, but there just aren't enough of them around. Running across one in a summer is about par for the course for us. Other people may have them around their flowers regularly, but they seem to boycott our place.

So it was all the more special finding one as we did—while we were gathering up rubbish.

We had been wandering around an otherwise delightful little park when we started noticing all the empty cans and bottles and wrappers lying about. As always, such thoughtlessness both irritated and baffled us. How can people enjoy such a beautiful place, and then leave it looking like a garbage dump? So, on our way out, we gathered up as much as we could carry, planning to take it home with us for proper disposal.

Near the car, however, we found a trash barrel we had not noticed earlier, so we deposited the rubbish there and decided to go back for more. That's when we were thanked by the hummingbird.

We were down by the stream, retrieving beer bottles, when the tiny hummer appeared at the opposite shore. It was no more than ten feet away, hovering at a tall, orange, wild lily. It posed obligingly for several moments. I don't think we've seen one that well in years (usually all we get is a glimpse out of the corner of the eye). The emerald green body. The long stickpin bill. The ruby patch on the throat. The blurred wings that create the "hum" of its name.

It was so enchanting we stopped muttering our unkind words about the people who had littered the park. We stood still, silently marveling, as the bird moved on to two other patches of lilies and then finally darted out of sight.

We had gone back for trash, and had found a jewel.

The only hummingbird I recall seeing last summer was one that nearly hit me as I walked through the backyard one evening. It came at

me so rapidly, and zoomed away so quickly, that just a moment later I wondered if I had really seen it at all.

Bettie had no trouble remembering her last hummer; it was outside a cabin we were visiting in Maine, three years ago.

Its rarity and its colorful appearance are only part of the hummingbird's charm. There are other unique qualities—such as size and personality—that also set it apart from other birds.

The rubythroat, which is the only variety of hummingbird in this part of the country, is so small it is often mistaken for a bumblebee or big moth. An adult weighs about the same as a copper penny. Its nest is the size of half a walnut shell. Its eggs are the size of peas, and newly hatched youngsters are so tiny a teaspoon will hold four of them.

But some other facts about the hummer are not small. For instance, its trick of hovering, helicopter-like, in midair burns up so much energy it has to eat almost constantly. One scientist who studied hummingbirds said that if a man spent as much energy as these birds, he would need a food intake of about 285 pounds of hamburger, or 370 pounds of boiled potatoes, or 130 pounds of bread just to break even. Every day.

Hummingbirds get all of this food from nectar in the flowers they visit, and from a wide assortment of insects and tiny spiders, so they have to stay on the go, from blossom to blossom. All day long.

However, while everything about the hummingbird seems to be in miniature, the bird doesn't seem to realize just how small it is. In its own heart, the hummer is an eagle.

When protecting its nest, the tough little hummer will dart out and rout all invaders, even kingbirds, which have earned a tough-guy reputation of their own by chasing away the much larger hawks and crows. But the kingbird won't stand up to the fury of a hummingbird.

When summer ends and cold weather is approaching, the humming-bird takes off for Central America. It flies thousands of miles on those two-inch wings, evading predators all the way, and can cross the 500 miles of the Gulf of Mexico nonstop. A marvelous little bird, indeed.

We talked about these things as we left the park. We wondered if planting honeysuckle, one of its favorite flowers, around the yard would bring hummingbirds close to the house. We talked of how we should look a little more closely for hummingbird nests, which we never have found, and how amusing it must be to see a hummer drive off a kingbird.

But mostly, we talked of how lucky we had been to see this hummingbird at all. We had already left the park when we returned to pick up rubbish. We felt well-paid.

29

Water Lilies

THE PEOPLE WHO dammed streams for their mills all those many years ago left us a legacy they probably never considered. Water lilies.

There are no better places to see the white-and-yellow—and occasionally pink—flowers than the quiet millponds: the shallow, still pools created by the stone-and-concrete dams. Long after the grinding of wheels was silenced, long after the buildings and the millers themselves vanished, the lilies remain.

In many cases, the plants are not appreciated. In fact, they are unwanted—often cursed—far more than they are praised. Water lilies tend to grow in dense colonies, and people who use the ponds for swimming or fishing resent the abundance of leaves that virtually cover the water's surface. I've complained about lily pads most in winter, when they mar the ice on a small pond where I like to skate.

But now, when the flowers are blooming, all is forgiven.

The ideal way to see the lilies is by drifting among the pads in a canoe or rowboat. You won't be able to paddle or row very fast, because the stalks beneath the pads get in the way, but a millpond in summer is not the kind of place to hurry through anyway. There may be ducks or muskrats swimming between the pads; both feed on the lily plants. Often you will see dragonflies resting or hovering there, flashing their iridescent blues or reds or greens or bronzes in the sunshine. Sometimes, little frogs are hunched up on the pads, waiting to snap up passing insects. And once in a while there may be a small bird—a rail, if you're lucky—probing its way across the pond, deftly stepping from pad to pad.

To get the most out of any water-lily show, go early. Not only are the attendant wild creatures most active early in the morning, but also the most impressive and fragrant of our native lilies is a mornings-only flower. Called simply the fragrant water lily, it is a gleaming-white blossom that rests directly on the water, next to its shiny foot-long pads. Shortly after sunrise, the flower unfolds gracefully, revealing numerous tapered petals around bright-yellow stamens and emitting a heady aroma. But by noon the flower has closed up shop for the day, with most of its perfume locked up tight as well.

There is another common water lily in our area, called the yellow pond lily. Its flower is far less spectacular—from a distance it looks like a yellow ball stuck on the end of a stalk. Years ago, when one of my sons was paddling through a millpond with me, he likened the yellow lily to the yolk of a hard-boiled egg, and I guess that's as good a description as any. However, its pads are special. Each is shaped like a heart, with a deep "V" notch at the base; as with most lily pads, these float on the water. The flower, on the other hand, often reaches above the surface, especially when the level of the water is low.

These days when I paddle around the ponds, I'm usually looking for special lilies, the pink ones. Perhaps it's only because I'm more conscious of them than of others, but it seems there are more pink lilies than there were in the past. They're still not plentiful, by any means, and it's

possible to search through a dozen ponds and thousands of flowers without finding one. But now I know of a few places where I can count on finding at least a handful of pink flowers each summer. Plant experts tell me there are two varieties of pink water lilies in our region. One is a mutation of the fragrant lily, mentioned above; the other is a descendant of a European plant introduced years ago as a decorative flower for goldfish ponds and other artificial pools. There are some subtle differences between the two pink lilies: The native has more petals; the European's petals are more rounded. As a general rule, you can be fairly sure the plant is native if it's growing in the wild. The European plant, which tends to grow in larger colonies, is more likely to be found in ponds in parks.

I prefer the native variety, but no matter whether native or introduced, whether white or yellow or pink, water lilies somehow epitomize the richness, the bounty, of summer. And on these mornings, when the world seems a little fresher, a little newer because of the lilies, we can thank something of old: the long-gone builders of millponds.

30

If I Could Order the Weather

Nοτ LONG AGO, on a cloudless, 85-degree afternoon, a friend slathered on suntan lotion and sighed, "If it were up to me we'd have weather like this every day."

That got me thinking. If I could order the weather, what would I want? Sunshine, day after day? Endless summer? No chance. Not for me, I find the changing seasons important, psychologically and emotionally, as well as physically and visually. For me, each change recharges the batteries, rekindles enthusiasm. It's almost as if each season provides a new start, a new segment of life.

Moreover, I would order a mixture of weather within each season. I prefer a few storms mixed in among the sunny days, partly because I simply like storms. Their combination of awesome beauty and unchained strength can be exciting, enchanting. And humbling.

In summer, I would order a couple of thunderstorms. Occasionally, I want to see the ominous boiling of black clouds in the afternoon. I want to hear the jarring thunder that seems to shake the ground. On a night or two, I want to see lightning flash wildly through the darkness, like some unleashed demon.

For the most part, I want cool, bright dawns freshly scrubbed with dew. A gentle rain, though, every now and then, would be needed, as much to soothe the nerves and make that five more minutes of sleep so precious, as to keep the countryside green and vibrant. And there would have to be showers once in a while during the day—there can be no rainbows without them—and we need banks of clouds in the west at dusk to provide colorful sunsets.

Summer nights should be starry, with a light breeze and little humidity, perfect for lingering outdoors. Of course, I'd also banish all mosquitoes and replace them with fireflies.

When summer had run its course, I'd welcome autumn's invigorating chill. I want the frosty dawns and foggy mists in the hollows and the migrating geese. I look forward to the winds that not only carry the aroma of wood smoke but also revive my spirit, calling me to wander over every hill and down every valley.

Autumn doesn't need many storms. Maybe around Halloween, I'd have a windy night when branches claw against the house and trees creak and moan, just to get in the mood.

Otherwise, I'd order sunshine to make the foliage more spectacular, and clear nights to keep the harvest moon bright and golden and friendly. And I'd make sure Indian Summer lasted for weeks—it's possibly my favorite of all periods.

Winter would start a few days before Christmas with a pristine blanket of snow, sort of a clean slate for the world. I'd want fresh snow to ski on, and thick, smooth ice to skate on. Most winter nights would be cloudless and still, so that I could marvel at the countless stars and intriguing constellations.

My order would include a couple of low-grade blizzards, too, complete with howling winds and deep, sculpted drifts. I'd want enough snow to make going to work or school unthinkable, but not enough to keep children from building snowmen and swooshing down hillsides.

Then it would be spring. Bird songs and apple blossoms and trilling frogs. Spring needs only two major changes—to begin earlier, and to last longer.

31

Cry of the Loon

DAYLIGHT IS FADING, and the fishing and canoeing are finished for the day. It's time to relax, to sit beside the campfire, swat mosquitoes and share quiet conversation. Twilight is a special time in the north woods.

Suddenly, a bizarre quavering wail shatters the solitude. Something like a fiendish laugh, it echoes across the smooth, darkening pond. Those unfamiliar with the country leap up, startled, and turn to each other: "Who, or what, was that?"

But it's not a monster or woods-crazed lunatic, though it sounds just like one. It's a loon. The voice of the wilderness. Mookwa, the "spirit of northern waters," as the Cree Indians long ago named it.

The first time they hear a loon calling, most people find it unnerving, chilling. Some say it's sad, or lonely. I consider it both stirring and poignant. The loon is indeed a symbol of untamed nature, and each time I hear it I feel privileged to be in a place where such creatures still exist. At the same time, the call is a warning that wild places are disappearing, and as they vanish, so do the truly wild animals.

Among wildlife, only the adaptable thrive. That's a sad statement, but true. Birds and other animals that can get along with people—the robins and mockingbirds, raccoons and squirrels—do very well. Those that insist on wildness, like wolves and bobcats, find themselves being crowded out. That's what's been happening to the loons for a long time now.

"Nearly every suitable lake within the breeding range of the species has its pair of loons, or has had it, and many large lakes support two or more pairs. The breeding range of this species is becoming more and more restricted as the country becomes cleared and settled; the loons are gradually killed off or driven away."

That lament was written more than 100 years ago, by one of New England's premier bird experts, Arthur Cleveland Bent. Bent was writing about Massachusetts, but today the same could be said about even the more remote New England states.

There are only a couple of hundred loons in Vermont these days, and the numbers are decreasing each year. New Hampshire's total has actually increased slightly in the last few years but only because of work

by the Loon Preservation Committee. Maine has most of our loons but there, too, they are moving farther north all the time, ever seeking out the more remote lakes and ponds.

When people move in, the loons usually move out.

Loons are goose-sized birds far more at home on water than on land. They often swim half submerged, with only their snaky neck and head above the water. They have unmistakable markings: green heads, bright-red eyes, black necks with a collar of white bars, white-flecked black backs and clear-white chests.

Voracious eaters of fish, loons are diving experts. Unusually heavy bones and an ability to squeeze air from their feathers enable loons to vanish below instantly and stay submerged far longer than most birds.

They can also cover a considerable distance beneath the surface—something that amazed me the first few times I came near one while I was canoeing on northern ponds. It became a game, trying to guess how far away and in which direction the submerged loon would reappear.

They've been around almost forever—at least 65 million years. That makes them one of the oldest species of bird. And maybe that's why they're so reluctant to change their ways to accommodate these new-comers called human beings.

Recently, though, there have been some signs that even loons are learning to adapt. Loss of nesting sites to pond-side construction has been one of the loons' biggest problems, but they have responded well in New Hampshire to a program that provides artificial floating islands for them to nest on.

In the Lake Winnipesaukee region in particular, the Loon Preservation Committee has had success combating the effects of development by building platforms and anchoring them offshore. These " islands" are squares made of cedar logs with wire mesh stretched across the middle; mud and shoreline vegetation are piled on the mesh to give the platforms a homey look for the loons.

Such programs do help, although it would be so much better if such steps were not necessary. Something is lost every time we have to "help" a wild creature.

Still, it's better to have the loons adapting to people—even if it seems as if they are selling out just a bit—than to not have them at all.

Just as long as they don't change that twilight cry. It is still the voice of the wilderness; the loon is still Mookwa, the spirit of the northern waters. If we lose the loon, we may have lost wilderness altogether.

32

We Almost Didn't Go

CHIPMUNKS. A MALLARD HEN and her brood. Blueberries. A defiant little turtle. Damselflies. Kingfishers. An oriole. Spiders. Geese. Quail. So much to see, and we almost didn't go.

I want to spend this particular morning, a Saturday, paddling my canoe around a large, "tame" pond near our house, but Saturday mornings being what they are, my favorite early hours slip by while I dally around home. And there is a heavy overcast, and I am a wee bit sluggish from late hours last night.

But the canoe is out, and if I stay home I'll wind up working in the garden, so why not? Almost as an afterthought, I ask Bettie to join me. She glances around at her own work and agrees to go. Only for two hours, she says.

We put in beside several fishermen, deciding to paddle the shoreline for a mile or so. Almost immediately, there is a chipmunk scurrying about in the bushes. It acts unafraid of us, and seems to be following our route. We wonder why, then notice another chipmunk about 30 yards ahead, heading our way. Perhaps they have a rendezvous planned. No, they pass each other by a few feet without stopping, each wrapped up in its own hectic little world.

A kingbird darts out from the treetops, attacking insects over the water. A gray squirrel is on the ground. Gypsy moths are fluttering about. A flicker is working on an ant hill. A grackle is bathing in the shallow water at the shore.

The shoreline here is almost park-like with so many paths created by the fishermen. Unfortunately, there also are far too many discarded cans and wrappers and other trash. Blueberry bushes lean out over the water, and the berries are plump and ripe. I go on shore briefly, find a paper cup, and Bettie quickly fills it with berries. For muffins, she says.

Two fishermen putt-putt-putt up in their motorboat, then cut their engine. One looks at our berries. "Maybe we'd be better off doing that," he says. No luck? I ask. "Not much, but there are fish in here, plenty of 'em, and big ones, too," he says. They drift away. Without blueberries.

The sun pops out, then plays peekaboo with the clouds. It's getting humid. Cicadas are droning, the first I've heard this year. Buttonbushes at the water's edge are "blooming" to the delight of bees. Pickerel weeds in the shallow coves are in flower, a deep purple. The last of the honeysuckle blossoms are still on, but already we see the first reddening leaves on a maple, a crippled sapling. A reminder of spring and a hint of autumn.

An oriole flashes by, its brilliant feathers a beacon against the greenery. Nuthatches and phoebes are calling from the trees. I see a small turtle resting among the pebbles in shallow water, reach down and pick it up. It's a young snapper, about three inches long. It pulls its legs inside the shell but opens its beaked mouth in silent defiance. Its eyes are glaring in anger, but it is really helpless. When I release it, it floats on the surface for a moment, then swims back to the bottom.

Through the clear water we can see a few slim sunfish, nearly motionless, and thick schools of tiny minnows. The scooped-out redds or nests from the spawning season are evident in the sandy areas. Also can see far too many beer cans and bait containers beneath the water. Already, most of the fishermen in boats and canoes are leaving. They, too, prefer the early hours.

Seven Canada geese fly by, low over the water, apparently a family heading for the far corner of the pond. Heard a pair had nested there. Blue damselflies are dancing over the water in pairs. Some sort of ritual? A tiger swallowtail butterfly, minus part of its tail, is working the buttonbushes along with the bees. A quail whistles in the distance. Two kingfishers in the shoreline trees rattle loudly as they flee from perch to perch.

A flat boat with "Marine Officer" on its side roars up. "You folks fishing?" asks the stern-looking warden. No, just paddling around. Why? "I'm checking fishing licenses. I see you have your life jackets, so you're in business. Have a good time." His demeanor changes a little—perhaps a hint of envy—and he is gone.

As we ride out the warden's wake, we see a female mallard duck with ten yellow-faced ducklings trying to hide beneath bushes at the shore.

Mama stays between us and her brood. She stretches out low, as close to the water as possible, as if trying to make herself disappear. The youngsters follow along very closely, moving as one. We swing wide to avoid panicking the nervous mother.

Bettie notices a tiny spider, apparently suspended in mid-air, as we paddle beneath overhanging branches. Put your paddle above it, I suggest. She does, and cuts the invisible thread. The spider was dangling about 12 feet down from a limb, at least 15 feet from shore. Probably awaiting a breeze so it could "fly" to some new territory.

A big group of beetle-like insects are zipping about on the water's surface, as if skating. More quail whistles come from the field behind the trees. A male mallard slips into thick vegetation and hides. A green heron flies from a high perch back into the woods, then screams a protest. An unseen mourning dove is uttering its plaintive call from somewhere in the forest.

Our two hours are already up, and we have not gone one-fourth the distance we had planned. We turn back toward the car. Other fishermen have arrived. One, still carrying his gear to the water, asks if we caught anything. He seems bewildered when we tell him we weren't fishing. His expression seems to say, why take a canoe out if you're not going to fish? We don't bother telling him.

33

The Swimming Hole

You grab a rope, steady yourself for an instant, then take a few running steps and launch into the air. A moment later, you let go of the rope and drop.

Instantly, the day's heat is forgotten. In fact, the water's chill is something of a shock to the system. But, oh, so refreshing.

The swimming hole. Every kid who grows up in the country has a favorite one. It may be a pond hidden in the woods, or a bend in the river, or maybe a deep pool caused by a dam in some rushing stream.

Whatever it is, the swimming hole is something special. It's a part of childhood, a place not likely to be forgotten.

Yes, I know parents frown on swimming holes these days. They're supposedly too dangerous—you seldom see lifeguards there—and often the water is less than pure. In some cases, it can be hard to know what lies beneath the water, the shoreline rocks can be jagged and there are always the possibilities of poison ivy nearby or broken glass in the area.

I know all that, but I still like seeing kids choose a swimming hole over a backyard pool. I even join them sometimes. It's simply more fun.

My own swimming hole years ago was in a languid, muddy river in another part of the country. The water was so murky we could hold our hands six inches beneath the surface and not be able to see them. The bottom was soft, squishy mud that felt even cooler than the water as it oozed between the toes. If we bumped into a hard object down there, it was more likely to be a snapping turtle than a rock.

New England's streams are much clearer and colder, but also much rockier. Nobody should dive headfirst into a stream or pond here without first checking out the water's depth and just what the bottom is like. A few tragic accidents seem to occur each summer because swimmers leap blindly into shallow water and strike rocks.

But long-established swimming holes are something else. Often, generations have been swimming in the same spots, swinging from ropes tied to the same trees, leaping off the same rocks, whooping it up with the same kind of exuberance. Such places are just as much fun now as they were in 1955 or 1925, or, for that matter, 1885 or 1785.

I especially like the deep pools in otherwise shallow, fast-running streams. There, water is cold enough even in midsummer to send shudders through you the first time you drop in. I know of a couple places where swimming holes were created in such streams by makeshift rock dams, much like stone walls, being built through the water. They make the pools deep enough for decent dips, and there is still enough current to keep the water cold and clean.

Even building or repairing a swimming hole dam is part of the fun— every kid loves to build dams—and there are other fringe benefits to choosing a pool in a river over one in the backyard. If you get tired or bored with swimming, you can prowl the shoreline looking for bullfrogs. You can try to catch dragonflies, or search for muskrat burrows, or see how many acorns you can shake down with each swing on the rope, or turn over rocks and watch crayfish scurry away.

Get a bunch of boys together, and sooner or later they will build a log raft. It may float half-submerged—mine usually did—and might be abandoned after a day or two, but that doesn't matter. Building it is the fun.

The adventurous may decide to make a diving board by nailing a plank to a tree limb. A few may wander down the stream in search of deeper pools or higher ledges from which to leap. Eventually, they'll be back, swinging on the rope.

Ask old-timers about their boyhood (or girlhood) swimming holes and they are likely to slip into long, nostalgic reminiscences. They won't remember the poison ivy, but they'll recall the scary yet thrilling rides on the ropes. They may not talk about mosquito bites, but they remember clearly how the cold water seemed to take their breath away. Scraped shins? Stubbed toes? Yeah, probably, but what a way to spend a summer afternoon!

Invariably, they will pause in conversations about swimming holes. They'll be thinking back to those summer afternoons of sunshine and cool water and youthful camaraderie. They'll be thinking about their own rafts and rock dams. They'll be thinking about a time when they felt totally free.

At swimming holes there are no rules except the rules of common sense. No limits on time or numbers in the water. And, perhaps best of all, no adults. Kids have always needed a few such escapes, probably more than they get today.

It's also certain the old-timers will soon be smiling. Maybe they no longer swing on ropes into swimming holes, but they haven't forgotten how it felt. It was a special time in a special place. Somehow, I can't picture kids who know only backyard swimming pools ever having that feeling.

34

A Liberated Sandpiper

Spotted sandpipers are little birds that hardly anybody notices. But they've suddenly become significant in our family. I don't think either Bettie or I will look at the sandpipers in quite the same way again.

For those unfamiliar with these birds, they are robin-sized stalkers of marsh edges and stream banks, bobbing along with a distinctive bouncing gait. I used to think they were merely interesting. Now I find they are something more—perhaps leaders of birddom's feminist movement.

Right now, I think they might be Bettie's favorite birds.

We've seen the sandpipers for years, almost every time we've taken the canoe out or strolled along a river, pond or marsh. They're fairly attractive birds, grayish or olive brown above, with white undersides sprinkled with freckles. They also have a white stripe along the edge of their wings that flashes when they fly.

Their flights are short. When flushed, the birds go only as far as necessary, around a bend or across the stream. And they fly so low they sometimes touch the water with their choppy wing beats.

Until now, what I found most intriguing about spotted sandpipers is the way they dance along the water's edge. Their tails bob so much that the birds are sometimes called teeter-tails. They remind me of teenagers sauntering down the street plugged into their radios; the sandpipers seem oblivious of the rest of the world, boogying to tunes only they can hear.

There is, however, more to these birds than idle dancing. They are a female-dominated species to a degree that's probably unparalleled among other New England birds. Female spotted sandpipers are not just liberated; they run the show.

To Bettie and me, house finches have long been the epitome of male chauvinism. Several pairs nest around our yard every spring, and it amuses me, and infuriates Bettie, the way the males perch somewhere and issue orders, never lifting a feather to help, while the females build the nests. Just the way life should be, I've said. Bettie hasn't exactly agreed.

But recently I stumbled across some information about spotted sandpipers, and now Bettie has her bird heroes, or heroines.

The female sandpipers are bigger and sometimes more heavily spotted than the males. In the spring, the females arrive first. The females establish territory, often fighting other females for desirable stretches of shoreline.

They then defend that territory against invaders. And the females take the lead in courtship.

It goes on. The females do lay the eggs, but more often than not they then leave the nest, and so the males are stuck with incubating the eggs and caring for the young. Why does the female leave? So she can mate with two or three more males and establish other happy homes. Only the last male, say the bird experts, gets much help in the care and feeding of baby sandpipers.

I think that's despicable. Bettie thinks it's only justice. Now when I see what I think is a female sandpiper, I call her a whole list of unflattering names. Bettie sees the same bird and says things like "Right on!" and "Go for it!"

She thinks it's about time there was a female bird in charge. She cites the house finches and the many other species in which the males make the decisions and then desert the nest. But I say that's different: How does that excuse the sandpipers? Whatever happened to motherhood?

A few weeks ago, Bettie's favorite birds were scarlet tanagers and orioles and bluebirds—all nice, sweet-voiced singers with ordinary lifestyles. Those males are the ones with the bright colors and pretty feathers; all they have to do is sing well and look good. Now Bettie goes out of her way to find sandpipers.

So we're spending more time in the canoe this summer than usual. And somehow I get the feeling this sandpiper liberation is starting to rub off.

Lately, I'm the only one doing any paddling.

35

Summer Twilight

IT'S A MAGICAL TIME, daylight sliding into darkness. Creatures of day giving way to creatures of night. The transition goes quickly. One hour.

The day has been hot and sticky, but the evening air offers some relief. On my way to the pond, I notice many people have left their air-conditioned houses. They are watering their lawns, walking dogs, just strolling. Tennis and basketball courts at the high school are busy. Traffic is heavy; where is everybody going?

I intend to take a long walk, but I get no farther than the pond. I pause to listen to a bullfrog bellowing from the weedy shoreline. I think how difficult it is to put into words a bullfrog's sound. Usually, I see it spelled "ha-rumpf" or "rarr-bit," but this one is more like "aye-yaw." Must be its New England accent.

The sun has not yet set, but has slipped behind clouds on the western horizon, turning those clouds a vivid purple. Clouds in the east are still white and wispy. The sky above, so clear and blue all day, has lightened considerably, but perhaps that's because of its contrast with the dark clouds in the west.

A month ago, summer was at its height and seemed endless. One month from now, autumn will be coming down the slope. Already, young maples at the water's edge show some of the colors of fall. Wild grapes are ripening. Yet, mosquitoes are buzzing around my ears and a dragonfly, as large as some of the birds in the brush, hovers a few inches from my face as it investigates this strange evening invader.

I feel I have one foot in summer, the other in autumn.

A small flock of geese flies over, already in a V-formation. It's too early for migration; are they just practicing? A couple of chimney swifts sail by, twisting and turning as they chase down insects. Then a barn swallow does the same.

Ripples gleaming silver in the sky's reflection reveal a large muskrat slowly making its way through the weedy shallows. It nibbles a bit here, tastes a sprig there, patiently meandering out toward deeper water. Eventually, it chooses a stalk of something—I'm too far away to tell what — and swims back with the plant trailing along behind.

A slight movement nearer shore catches my eye. A small, slim duck is there: a female wood duck. I find myself shaking my head in bewilderment. The woodies have done it to me again. Each spring I see wood ducks shortly after they arrive—the males are among the most brilliantly colored of all birds—but then they vanish. Each year, I'm sure they have moved on to other nesting places, but each August they show up again, often with half-grown youngsters.

There is no movement in the air; leaves are hanging limp and lifeless. The water is just as still. Frequently, I see tiny disturbances, mere dimples in the surface, as insects touch down. That leads to larger circles as fish rise to feed. If the insects are mosquitoes, I hope the fish are eating their fill.

In half an hour, the birds begin settling down. There are some blue jays jabbering in the distance but few other calls. Now I can hear a dog barking somewhere, a truck shifting gears on a hillside, a plane droning high overhead. The kingfisher is perched on a dead branch over the water, silhouetted against the sky. I'm not sure I've ever seen a kingfisher this quiet before—they're usually screaming about the fish they caught, or about one that got away—but this bird seems to be waiting for darkness. After several minutes, it suddenly dives toward the water, pulls up at the last moment, then flies off toward the woods. Gone.

By now, the shoreline trees and hills beyond seem to loom larger, casting dark reflections into the water. Only the center of the pond remains light, and the water surface there takes on a silvery sheen. The sun has set, leaving the clouds in the west a deep, ominous blue-black.

Despite the gathering darkness, I can see more wood ducks gliding silently out of the weeds and bushes: two near me, another one well out from shore, then a flock—probably a family—of six in the midst of the water lilies. And to think I didn't know there were any wood ducks in this pond.

A large white moth flutters by, just above the water. More bullfrogs have joined the original one, and I find each one's call distinctive. Something disturbs the redwings in the bushes, and a male flies out crying a protest, but all quickly calms down again. I hear a frog lunge through the water just below me; maybe it caught the white moth.

It's dark enough now that only a small patch of water is visible, but the fish are becoming more active; now I can hear their rises as well as see them. Car lights appear on the far side of the pond, and for a moment I think somebody is coming to try to catch catfish. I quickly realize it's more likely the car belongs to young lovers. The lights go off instantly.

Mosquitoes are making it difficult to remain, so I start for home. A few fireflies are winking over the bushes. A cicada is droning from the woods. I listen hard for the owls I know haunt the hillside, but they are silent tonight. There are no bird sounds at all.

Traffic has diminished only slightly. Action is heavy around the lemonade and ice cream stands. Many moths are crowding around each street light. The tennis court is dark and deserted. A lone figure is still on the basketball court; he must be shooting by feel as much as by sight.

There are no stars out; the only lights in the overcast sky are those of two airplanes. I walk on through the darkness, thinking about the kingfisher and the muskrats and the wood ducks and the dragonfly and the bullfrogs. In one hour, I watched a day end and a night begin. I try not to think about all the mosquito bites.

36

The Initial Tree

BEECH TREES ARE SPECIAL. I know I've said that about a lot of trees—hemlocks, sycamores, hickories, hollies, swamp maples and certain oak trees. They're all special to me in one way or another.

But none of the others evokes the same feelings in me as the beeches: admiration and guilt. In almost equal proportions.

Most people know the beech. It's the tall, broad, straight tree of the old forests and parks. The one with the remarkably smooth gray bark. The one covered with carved initials and dates and hearts.

It's hard to find a mature beech with an uncarved trunk. There's something about that bark that apparently is irresistible to a kid with a pocketknife or a young man trying to impress his girl. Long before I learned that the tree's name is beech, I knew it as "the initial tree." Whenever we found a beech, we'd check it for the oldest date, and then would add our own initials and the date of our visit. At the time, I never questioned what we did—that's what beeches were for. Maybe we were trying to achieve some sort of immortality, trying to show that we had indeed passed this way.

Of course, there were times when I cheated a little. I remember once, probably during the 1950s, when I tried to fool my brothers with a beech carving. I had discovered an immense beech, a majestic relic, far back in our woods. There were only a few sets of initials on it, carved so long ago they could not be deciphered. The tree seemed ancient to me—at least a couple of hundred years old—so an idea quickly hatched in my devious mind.

I reached up as high as I could and carefully carved, "A. Wayne,

1776." You have to remember that this was in Ohio, and General Anthony Wayne, "Mad Anthony," was a hero to every schoolboy in the area. He had defeated the Indians in the Battle of Fallen Timbers, not far from our farm, and to have found his initials on one of our trees would be seen as a major coup. I rubbed dirt into the letters and numbers to make them look old, and then left my handiwork.

Perhaps a month later, I invented some excuse for luring my brothers into that section of the woods so that they would share in my "discovery." The ruse wasn't too successful. Even the dirt couldn't make a month-old carving look 175 years old, and I was immediately accused. My brothers knew me too well— who else would have fouled up history so much?

A. Wayne, I was informed, was busy elsewhere in 1776. Something called the Revolutionary War. It wasn't until the 1790s that he was sent to Ohio to fight the Indians. I was reminded of that blunder often in the following years, and I soon stopped wandering in the vicinity of that tree.

Carving my own initials also lost its appeal eventually, but my admiration for the splendid trees remained intact. Now, I quietly rejoice when I find an unmarked beech—there are so few of them—and I cringe just a little each time I see a fresh set of letters on an old tree. Beeches are too beautiful to be disfigured, and I deeply regret having taken part in such a practice—even when I got the dates right.

Southern New England has far more beeches than Ohio, and a grove of the trees can be a delightful place. In spring and early summer, the leaves are a refreshing light green, almost a pastel, that creates the aura of a tranquil glen. Often, there are nearby boulders to sit on, and perhaps a gurgling brook to dangle your feet in. Just the kind of place to linger— the kind of place mosquitoes wouldn't dare enter.

In fall, beech leaves become golden, setting the entire grove aglow when caught by the sunshine. Many of the leaves cling to the trees through the winter, becoming brown and leathery, similar to those on oak trees. Walk through a beech grove in winter, before there is snow, and the leaves that have fallen crackle underfoot. It's almost like walking on potato chips.

Beech trees also produce beechnuts, of course, which are edible. Squirrels and chipmunks usually beat us to the triangular nuts—hearing those hoarders frantically scrambling around in the beech leaves is a familiar sound in late autumn and early winter. I've always wondered how the squirrels and chipmunks know just when the prickly outside cases will split to reveal the nuts. Do they check them every day?

Anyway, I finally found reasons to appreciate beech trees beyond their bark, and now I try to teach my sons to leave their knives in their pockets when they find a beech. There are other ways to let the world know you were here, other ways to proclaim undying love for that special girl. Don't ask the beech tree to do it.

Also, there are other ways to play tricks on your brothers . . . and to show why you flunked history.

37

Catfish

EVERYBODY KNOWS THE time to go fishing is early in the morning. Except, that is, when you're after catfish. Then you go in the evening. Twilight time is catfish time.

I know, most people will ask, Why would you want to catch catfish? They're ugly, only so-so fighters and have those wicked barbs on their heads that make taking the hooks out a bit dangerous for the fisherman. Why bother with something like that when you could be fishing for trout or bass?

Well, you either like going for catfish or you don't. Those who specialize in trout or bass won't understand. If fly-fishing for rainbows or brookies in a swift stream is your game, patiently waiting beside a slow-moving river for a catfish to hit your worm will seem tame. If tangling with an enraged large-mouth bass you've lured out of a weed bed is what you consider the only way to fish, you're not going to get excited about reeling in a catfish that only halfheartedly tugs at your line.

No, catfishing is not for the masses. It's for those who go fishing for more than fish.

A few times every summer, my boys and I go after catfish. We've found two or three spots that are pretty dependable: deep holes in a sluggish and otherwise shallow river.

It isn't necessary to come back with a mess of fish to have a successful evening at the river. It took me a while to realize it, but perhaps catfish aren't the reason I join the boys, who are the real fishermen in the family. The fish are just a good excuse to be there, on the riverbank, as twilight deepens.

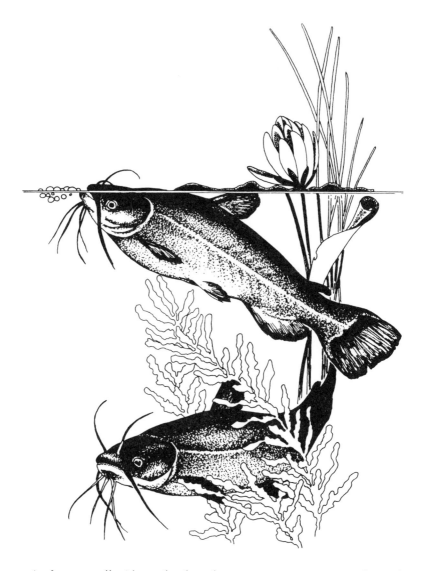

At first, we talk. About the day, about our current projects, about the level or the turbidity of the water. Maybe we mention the mosquitoes. Sometimes, we even talk about catfish. But as the evening wears on, each of us settles into his own thoughts. Boys don't mention things like orange streaks in the western sky, or katydids scratching out their monotonous three notes from the woods, or the magical lighting of the stars and planets as darkness falls. But I know they notice.

We don't even talk much about the other happenings—the night call of a heron, the gleaming V-shaped wake of a swimming muskrat, the sonorous bullfrog in the weeds, the crazy flight of a passing bat. We simply absorb it all. Inevitably, one of the boys will decide we don't really need the lantern, and so we'll fish under the moon and stars, except when baiting hooks or removing a fish from a hook. They won't say that artificial light interferes with the charm of the deepening night, but nobody has to. We all understand.

I haven't asked them, but I doubt the boys brag to their friends about the catfish we catch. They would rather talk about bass, even the ones that got away, and now they are learning fly-fishing, so trout are becoming important to them.

But every so often, they still suggest heading down to that muddy river for an evening of catfishing. Whenever possible, I join them. There aren't many better ways to end a summer day.

38

The Scythe

SMOOTH AND STEADY. Smooth and steady. Swing and step. Swing and step. Develop a rhythm. Easy does it. No wild hacking. No wasted motion.

At first, I have to run the procedure through my mind. But only for a few moments. Then I fall into the rhythm, and the work progresses almost effortlessly. The scythe's blade flashes in the sun. A swath of weeds falls. I step forward, the blade flashes again, more weeds fall. It's almost as if my arms and shoulders, back and legs, are part of a machine. It becomes harder to stop the rhythm than to continue.

Maybe it's a sign of age creeping up on me, but old-fashioned things like the scythe appeal more as time goes by. Over the years I've collected quite a number of obsolete tools, most of them for farming, just because I like their simplicity: the gadget that sowed wheat and oats several generations ago, for example, or the corn planter.

I don't use the corn planter or wheat broadcaster. I don't have a farm, for one thing, and anyway they would be too slow even for me. But I cherish them, just as I do the other hand tools I've accumulated: ice saws, augers, broad axes, pitchforks. They tell me of other people and other times. They were used by the men and women who helped build this nation, possibly some of my own ancestors. I like that feeling of linking up with the past.

The scythe, when I bought it at a barn sale, was meant to be just another part of my collection. I probably bought it because it has the longest blade of any scythe I'd ever seen—37 inches—and the wooden shaft is gracefully curved. It's a piece of art, perfect for hanging on my

basement wall.

But it didn't stay on the wall long. When summer came, I discovered there were weeds beyond the garden that I couldn't cut with the power mower; the ground there was too rough. I whacked the weeds off once with a hand sickle—another relic—and then decided to try the scythe.

It wasn't particularly easy to use. The secret is swinging it so that the blade remains horizontal, parallel to the ground. With a 37-inch curved blade, that's no snap. I slammed the blade point into the ground more times than I care to remember before I got the hang of it. When all the movements finally came together, I felt like I had really accomplished something. One giant step—backward—for mankind.

It's not like I had never seen a scythe before buying this one. We had one on the farm I grew up on, stored up in the barn loft with all the other "junk" we no longer used. Eventually, these hand tools were sold to some city people looking for antiques. My parents were only too glad to get rid of them—those tools didn't mean the "good old days" to them; they meant hard work.

My brothers and I felt the same way. We couldn't wait to trade in the crosscut saw for a chain saw, the spade for a Rototiller, the corn knife for a tractor-mounted corn picker.

So I'm not really sure how to explain the satisfaction I feel when swinging the scythe. Maybe it's as another ex-farmer once wrote, that power tools leave a man mentally tired and physically tense, whereas a good hand tool leaves a man physically tired and mentally relaxed.

I am sure the scythe would lose its appeal if I had to use it for mowing an entire hayfield. But to go out and level weeds a few times each summer, it's just right.

39

The Insect Orchestra

SCREECHING, SCRATCHING AND RASPING. Droning, buzzing and fiddling. Chirping, shrilling and scraping. It's quite a racket, a big noise. And it's made by tiny creatures.

This is the insects' time. This is when they fill the nights with their sounds. Usually, it's midsummer that is thought of as insect time, when on hot nights we first hear the insect chorus; but right now, as August melts into September, the sound is turned up to full volume. It's almost as if the bugs had suddenly realized that their time is dwindling, and they are trying to get in as much activity as possible before cool weather slows them down—frost will silence them altogether.

Grasshoppers and crickets make up two major sections of this nocturnal, virtually all-male orchestra. Cicadas are noisy too, although they are basically day bugs. And just about now the loudest player, the star of the show, is tuning up: Katydids are adding their "fiddles" to the din, and you know what that means. According to folklore, when katydids start screeching, first frost will arrive in six weeks.

I doubt that katydids can predict the weather any better than groundhogs, but just hearing them out there in the night drives home a point. No matter how hot and humid these nights may be, summer is fraying around the edges and fall is starting to loom.

The katydid is a green grasshopper-type insect, with a built-in fiddle. The insect creates its monotonous three-note sound the same way a cricket does its chirping: by drawing one rasp-edged wing across the other. Somebody, way back when, likened the sound to "Katy did," but others insist the lyrics are, or should be, "frost is near" or "six more weeks." In this area, katydids are usually a little early; they start screeching by mid-August, so six more weeks would put first frost around the beginning of October. That happens occasionally, but more often there are no hard frosts here until at least the middle of October.

Anyway, the katydid is only one member of this bizarre group of noise makers. Some have been with us all summer; others have just recently reached maturity and joined the union. It would take an entomologist to identify them all, even by sight. There are what experts call true katydids and false katydids, and there are numerous varieties of crickets and grasshoppers, along with lesser-known cousins of both of those families. Almost nobody sees them; they are just sounds in the darkness. Very loud sounds.

How loud? Katydids and cicadas supposedly can transmit their sounds a full mile. Both carry their own complex amplifiers. The katydid's amplifier, less than an eighth of an inch long, balloons a tiny scratch into the *zeep* note that can be heard a mile away. The amplifier is made of chitin, the same stuff that forms the shells of most insects, and scientists assert that though it is thinner than paper, it is stronger than comparably thick steel.

The cicadas' sound system is even more complicated. These thick-bodied bugs create their buzzing by vibrating "drumheads" called timbals inside cavities in their abdomens. They regulate the volume by opening and closing plates that cover the cavities, bouncing the noise off sounding boards and then letting the air swell the buzzing to a level that almost hurts human ears. It's a complex system for such a monotonous sound, but it must be effective; cicadas have used it to maintain the species for eons.

In addition, grasshoppers and crickets are out there fiddling around every night. A grasshopper stands on its "hands" and draws a "bow"— one of its big back legs—across a line of small stiff pegs on the wing. The sound is often likened to the grinding of an all-but-dead battery. Crickets similarly rub a scraper on the left wing against a file on the right to produce their *Creeak! Creeak!*

The purpose of all this noise is, of course, the same as with the frogs' bellowing in the spring. Courtship. Time really is running out for the insects, many of which will be killed by the frost, and so these males are urgently seeking females, which then have to lay their eggs so that another generation of screechers and scratchers and scrapers will be around next summer.

It can't be easy for the females to decide on suitors, picking out one sound from the raucous multitude. And some females have extra difficulty. Take the tree cricket: The male is extremely loud, and persistent, but the female is totally deaf. Still, love will find a way; the male's enthusiastic fiddling produces a fluid that has an odor the females can't resist.

So this bizarre band plays on. Far into the night. Every night. Each member is doing its own thing, creating its own music. Hundreds of thousands of males wooing hundreds of thousands of females.

Only cold will stop them now. And anybody who listens to this orchestra will know how silent the winter nights really are.

40

The Fogs of Dawn

You HAVE TO be an early riser to see them, but signals of autumn's approach are moving in. The fogs of dawn are reminders that summer is not endless after all.

I suppose most people don't want to be reminded of autumn—end of vacation, back to school, close up the beach house and summer cottage—but I look forward to September, so I welcome the fogs of dawn.

Drive by a pond or stream these days just after daybreak and you can see the fogs, light, wispy clouds just above the water. They swirl about, playing tag with the breezes, then seemingly shiver the instant sunshine reaches them over the treetops. For a moment, they gleam in the sunshine, all sparkles and glitter, and then they are gone.

Hal Borland, a kindred spirit who spent the last 35 years of his life on a farm in Connecticut, called the late-August fogs "the incense of fading summer."

Borland also wrote: "This is the shimmery gauze of the changing season, the dew which washes the dust from the summer-weary leaves along the streams and keeps green the valleys beyond the season's prime. This is the blown breath of autumn long before there is even a hint of frost in the air."

August nights, of course, are among the hottest of the year. The air seems to weigh heavily on the land. Many nights are humid and sticky. Cicadas drone and crickets scratch and moths flutter at the lights. People without air conditioning can find sleeping difficult. Summer, indeed, seems endless.

But by dawn there are changes. Somewhere in the night, a bit of chill sneaks in for a few hours, and that brings the fogs. It can be 90 degrees again by noon, but in those early hours we can see September coming. The air above the water is cooled just enough to create the filmy, white mists, and to assure us that the seasons are still progressing on schedule. For now, for me, that is enough.

Autumn is my favorite season, and has been since I discovered what fall in New England is like. Spring here is too short, winter too long, and summer often too humid and draining. I'm always ready for summer to end, for autumn to begin I wouldn't mind if fall lasted a few extra months. It is invigorating, both physically and spiritually. The woods and hills and streams again become inviting—in fact, irresistible—with spectacular colors and tantalizing aromas and tugging breezes. Do others find these lures impossible to ignore? I do. In autumn, I have to get out and go.

Obviously, the fogs we find these mornings don't mean that autumn is here, but they are the hint, the warning. Even flipping the calendar page to September doesn't automatically bring autumn, but now we know it is coming. Fall is floating toward us on the river, waiting there on the pond. We may or may not be ready for autumn yet, but that doesn't matter. It will come whether we are ready or not.

The fogs of fall arrive earlier in the North Country, of course. Those who vacation on ponds or lakes in Maine, New Hampshire or Vermont probably know these fogs well, unless they sleep 'til noon. The fogs begin settling over the water in early August, and on particularly cool mornings they can be so thick you feel you have to push your way through. I remember a canoe trip in northern Maine in August during which we purposely broke camp very early each morning just to enjoy the dense fog. Paddling through it was an eerie, intriguing experience, and watching it glimmer and then melt away in the sunshine was certainly worth losing a couple hours of sleep.

Now, the fogs are coming here. They will appear more regularly in weeks ahead. They will become thicker and last longer. Before long, they won't be restricted to the watery places, but will lie in each wooded hollow, then in the low meadows, pastures and fields. Eventually, they will begin arriving by evening and won't dissipate until almost midday. By then, trees will be aglow with red, gold and orange, and birds will be in restless flocks, preparing for the long flights South. Autumn will be here.

But that is several weeks down the road. It is still August, and for those who cherish summer, there is still time for beaches and swimming and the other things of summer. Frost and migrating geese are a long way off. Yet, even the most enthusiastic summer people ought to realize their season is approaching its end. Autumn is on its way; the fogs of dawn are the proof.

41

September

September arrived during the night, and that means more than simply flipping a page on the calendar. September is more than a new month, it is a new season. One of the best.

By a new season, I don't mean autumn. That's still a few weeks away, by the calendar and usually by the weather. No, September is a season all by itself, perhaps the season between summer and fall. A season of change, of newness, of revitalization.

September brings with it an invigorating freshness as the thick, oppressive air of summer is replaced by cooling breezes. And as soon as the air cools, even a little, the restlessness returns.

It is this restlessness, this wanderlust, of September that I find so irresistible. It pulls me away from the house, away from garden chores and yard work, and practically forces me to climb the hills and roam the fields and float the rivers again. I call it fall fever, and it seems to hit harder each year. Sometimes it lasts only a few weeks; often it doesn't run its course until well into November. But it starts now, in September.

I've long been convinced that fall fever, the urge to be out and moving, is the reason hunters and trappers and explorers ranged so far at this time of year. They probably offered other reasons—more game, prime pelts—but I'm sure that certain something in the September breeze had about as much to do with it. Perhaps fall fever is why men still hunt, a plausible reason to be out tromping through the woods and wandering the fields. The breezes say there is something new, something exciting, just around the next bend, just over the next ridge. Keep going.

Birds, of course, are great examples of the restlessness of September.

Many are in loose flocks already, long before time to migrate south. They flit about the countryside, from meadow to woods to pasture, as aimless as wind-blown leaves. They seem to know it's not time to migrate just yet, but they cannot sit still. September is calling.

It's easy to notice that call—something of a call of the wild—being heard by dogs. Watch virtually any dog when the first cooling breezes waft down from the hillsides, and you'll see a longing, far-away gaze in its eyes. It may never have spent a day hunting, but nearly every dog will begin straining at its leash, eager to run through the forest, to dash and leap alongside invisible ancestors that were their own masters. My old dog, which spends most of the summer snoozing beneath a shady spruce, acts years younger each September. Once more, he wants to chase every squirrel, to climb every ledge, to explore every trail.

Since I feel the same, we go off together. He's the ideal companion; we understand each other. With him, I don't have to explain why I suddenly drop the garden tools and wander down to the stream. He never asks why a guy my age scrambles up rock outcroppings. It's perfectly okay with him if I want to walk the same long woods lane three evenings in a row. He'll go too; he hears the same call.

What do we see? Maybe a flock of wood ducks hiding in a tiny cove. Or a raccoon in the grape vines, its face purple from the juicy fruit. Or a muskrat rebuilding a lodge, or a chipmunk with its cheeks bulging with acorns, or one branch of a maple in riotous orange while the rest of the tree is still green, or a Virginia creeper vine lighting up a dead tree as if ablaze.

If we go out at dawn, I say I want to find the fox we heard yipping last night. Or I'll go out on a moonlit night, hoping to catch a glimpse of the great horned owl that hunts over the pasture. Foxes and owls are good excuses for walks.

But it really doesn't matter much what we see; it's just being out there that counts.

Now, it seems, we can walk for hours. Trails that wore us out in July are no problem at all. By the time we return, I might not remember all the places we went or just what we saw, but I know the hours were well-spent. Even if the feet are weary, the spirit is refreshed. And satisfied.

Until that tantalizing breeze starts blowing again.

42

Mount Oops

In THE WOODS of northern Maine, miles from roads and villages, stands a rocky old mountain with a new name. The name, Mount Oops, doesn't appear on any maps, and probably never will, but I think it will become part of one family's lore.

The father and a son, then 18, had gone to the area to fish and canoe in the cool, clear ponds and rivers. They wanted some time together before the young man went off to college. They hadn't planned on climbing mountains, Oops or any other.

They were camping in a sheltered little cove, fishing from shore, after a day spent battling the wind-whipped waters of the pond. The wind continued raging through the treetops and howling around the mountains above.

Maybe it was the mountains' long shadows reaching over the pond that caught their fancy. Maybe it was the way the rocky tops glowed in the setting sun. Maybe it was just that the idea of climbing a mountain suddenly seemed more fun than fighting the wind and waves.

Whatever the reason, they decided that night, while listening to far-off loons, that they would forgo fishing for climbing. They discussed which peak to tackle, and finally chose a bald-topped knob that promised panoramic views of the entire region. There was another peak, probably just as high, a bit closer to the pond, but it had more trees on top, and they wanted the open views.

They knew there would be a problem. There were no trails up the mountain, and in the dense forest they wouldn't be able to see the summit for hours. How to determine just where to climb without a compass?

They made rough calculations from the bottom and started up.

It was hard going. The slope was steep and littered with fallen trees and decaying logs and slippery rocks. But it was beautiful, too. There were dense stands of waist-high ferns. Gleaming white flowers called bunchberries grew in profusion. Tiny brooks tumbled down the rocks.

The men followed deer trails at times. They saw signs of moose and porcupine. Red squirrels and chipmunks scolded them. Unseen grouse rocketed through the brush. Father and son hoped—sort of—they would come across a bear.

A rock wall—at first, they thought it was the summit—at last gave them a chance to get above the trees. Finally, they could see the top, only a couple of hundred yards away. Another deep ravine and a sharp incline lay ahead. They circled the steepest slope, discovered a rocky backbone of the mountain, and scrambled up.

The view was everything they'd expected. They could see many miles in all directions, thousands of acres of woods and ponds. They could see one small village, but no other houses. No roads.

They sat and marveled, talking about how they could be the first people ever to be on that rock. It wasn't likely, but they wanted to think that. A raven flew by, below them, squawking loudly. There was no other noise, nothing except the wind. It was a good place to be.

Except for one thing.

The son realized it first, about the time the father gave him the honor of naming their mountain. So it became Mount Oops.

Yep, they had started up one mountain and ended on another. They found it bewildering and amusing and a little embarrassing. So I won't reveal their names. I promised my son that much.

43

Warbler Confusion

Hᴇʀᴇ'ꜱ ᴀ ꜰʀɪᴇɴᴅʟʏ ᴛɪᴘ for anybody thinking of becoming a birder: Don't start in the fall. In particular, don't start by trying to identify the warblers that migrate through here in autumn. You're likely to become so frustrated you'll chuck the whole bird-brained idea.

Sure, there are some good birding activities available in fall—seeing the massive flights of hawks is one that shouldn't be missed—but the tiny warblers are something else. To people like me, who are only casual birders, nearly all of the warblers look alike. Apparently, some people can tell a hooded warbler from a Wilson's warbler at a glance, even in September, but I'm a little suspicious of people like that. They must have spent most of their lives studying the minute differences between the birds.

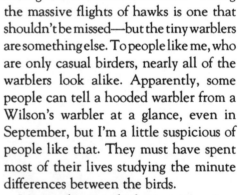

It's tough enough for me in spring, because warblers seldom sit long enough for me to get a good look at them. But at least when they come through in May they wear more distinctive colors than in September. In May, I might be able to identify a black-throated blue warbler, because then it is basically blue, with a black throat. And a chestnut-sided warbler is rather easy to figure out in spring, with its chestnut-colored streaks down each side.

But not now. Most warblers just don't play the game very fairly. They appear for only a few weeks in the spring, disappear for a couple of months, and then come hurrying through again in early autumn. And when they come back, they look so different.

In fall, it seems, all the warblers are brown and yellow. And we're not talking about four or five varieties of warbler; there must be three dozen, all easily confused. On top of that, many immature birds are involved in the migration, and they don't look the same as their parents. Real birders consider sorting out the fall warblers a challenge, a test of their expertise. It drives me crazy.

When somebody can talk me into looking for fall warblers—which isn't often anymore—I carry along a field guide. I figure, if Roger Tory Peterson can't point out the differences, then the situation is hopeless. And even Peterson admits that warblers are no snap; his book devotes several pages to colored paintings of "confusing fall warblers" in an attempt to specify what to look for. They all look alike to me.

Peterson breaks the massive clan into two general groups: those with streaks, or bars, on the wings, and those with plain wings. That should help, but it's hardly enough.

The other day, I saw a nondescript brownish warbler with faint white bars on its wings; it had very little yellow, for a change. Maybe I can get this one, I thought.

Out came Peterson's book, and I flipped to the page for "confusing fall warblers" with wing bars. For as long as the bird stayed in view, I alternately stared at it through binoculars and studied the paintings in the book. I'm still confused. It looked like something called a blackpoll, but it also looked like a Cape May warbler; of course, it could have been an immature pine warbler, or a young bay-breasted warbler. Maybe it was a ruby-crowned kinglet, which isn't a warbler at all; it just looks like one at this time of year.

The warblers without wing bars are no easier. Hooded warblers and Wilson's warblers look identical to me, now that the black "hood" of the former has been removed until next spring. Even with the book in hand I can't tell the difference between Connecticut warblers and mourning warblers. Right now, an immature Nashville warbler looks the same to me as the female yellowthroat, one of our more common warblers through-out the summer. At least the male yellowthroat is easy to identify; it wears a large black mask. As kids, we called it the Lone Ranger bird.

Ludlow Griscom, former research ornithologist at Harvard, spent more than 50 years studying warblers. Back in the 1950s, he edited a giant book called *Warblers of North America*. In it, he wrote, "The fall migration of warblers is by far the most fascinating, as well as the most difficult and sporting proposition."

Griscom said that identifying even the spring warblers requires "great physical energy, exceptional hearing ability, a ready and retentive memory for detailed facts instantly available, and a fund of enormous patience."

I'm afraid I fall short in nearly all categories.

I don't want to work that hard. And I like my birds to be more dependable than warblers. Other birds change feathers, or molt, too, but they don't wear disguises. Bluebirds don't turn green. Kingfishers are always the same colors. A wood thrush has the same markings in September as

it had in May. A migrating Canada goose doesn't try to look like a snow goose.

So I'll go looking for the hawks when they start down the coastline. I'll go out of my way to see the swallows congregate before their flight south. I'll probably stop by the ponds to see what ducks are passing through. I might even notice when the catbirds leave, and the juncos arrive. But I think the warblers are going to have to get along without me. They just don't play fair.

44

Fire in the Treetops

THE FIRST FIRES of fall are already ignited. They are sweeping up certain trees, blazing their way to the highest branches, threatening to set entire forests aflame.

Sound ominous, don't they?

Not to worry. These fires are only the leaves of a vine called the Virginia creeper—one of the first plants to switch from green to bright autumn colors.

When autumn approaches, people who attempt to describe the New England foliage inevitably liken the color show to fire raging through the forest. It's overdone, I know, but it's difficult to gaze at a swamp maple at the peak of its colors and not think of the scene as fiery. And who can look over a hillside of hardwoods glowing orange and gold and red without the word "ablaze" coming to mind?

It all starts with the Virginia creeper. It's an obscure, virtually unnoticed vine all during the summer; but by mid-September, it is impossible not to notice it. Almost overnight, the leaves turn scarlet, while most other plants are still summer green. Each fall, I think of flames shooting up a tree when I see the first creeper vine all in red. It's a cliche, but it never seems to change.

Some people confuse the Virginia creeper with another vine that turns bright colors in fall—poison ivy—but that shouldn't happen. For

one thing, creeper leaves occur in groups of five, whereas poison-ivy leaves are in threes. The leaves of the two plants also have different shapes, and the ivy berries are a dull gray, not lively blue, like the creeper's.

Anyway, there is not really that much to worry about. There is no need to touch the plants. The leaves are to look at and admire, not to gather. In fact, a Virginia creeper in its autumn finery is probably most impressive when viewed from a few yards away.

Virginia creeper crawls up other supports besides trees, of course—fences, stone walls, even some buildings—but it is on trees that I think the vine is most striking in fall. Actually, I'm even more picky than that;

I prefer to look for the creeper on dead trees. Tall dead trees. The taller and older the tree, the better.

On such trees, a Virginia-creeper vine seems to restore a bit of life. That's the case with an ancient oak at the foot of a hillside near my home. It has been dead for years; all the bark is gone. Wind and ice and time have taken their toll—the tree is scarred and tattered. More branches fall every winter, and after each storm I expect to see the entire tree lying on its side. It has to happen before long.

But somewhere in the past, a Virginia creeper attached itself to the oak's trunk and started growing. Perhaps a bird that had eaten a creeper berry elsewhere perched in the tree and dropped a seed; that's the way it usually happens. The seed sprouted into that vine, which is now thick and long, winding all the way to the very top of the oak. Sometimes I think it is only the vine that keeps the tree standing. I know it is the creeper's leaves that light up the tree each fall, enabling the old relic to take part in the autumn foliage display one more time.

So, a few times every September, I go looking. Sometimes I'm a little too early, and the tree is not yet "on fire." But the time always comes when I see the leaf clusters suddenly scarlet, burning through the morning mist, and then I feel a deep satisfaction.

I'm a fall person. I look forward to autumn with great anticipation, and the Virginia creeper's coloring signals the start of my favorite season. Apparently I share the restlessness of wild creatures; when fall comes, I have to get out and go. To see and hear and smell and feel this new season.

In New England, as perhaps nowhere else, the color is a major, vital part of the season. Asters and goldenrod aglow in the meadows; sumac in the waste places. A little later, the trees catch fire—the dogwoods and gums and beeches and birches and, of course, the maples. Color everywhere: crimson and orange and gold.

And all are ignited by the flames of a vine ignored the rest of the year. Something called the Virginia creeper.

45

Finally, Our Own Apples

THE OLD APPLE GROWERS who lived in my part of the state can rest easy now. Even though most of their orchards are gone, their spirit is alive in my yard. I'm doing my part in keeping the name Apple Valley true.

Any day now, I'll go out back and harvest this year's crop. Both apples.

Hey, don't laugh. Two apples is two more than I've ever gotten from my yard. Picking those two apples will be a proud moment for me.

For generations, the place where our house stands was an apple orchard. That wasn't unusual for this area; there were more apple trees than people or chickens or even oak trees on these hillsides back then. But the years took their toll on both the trees and their owners. It was easier, and more profitable, to grow subdivisions and condos than to plant trees.

When we bought our place, there were no apple trees on it; in fact, no fruit trees of any kind. The previous owner cared more about flowers and shade than fruit. Almost immediately, we began replacing many of his trees with our own, and have been picking peaches and cherries and plums for many years now. But no apples.

It must have been a dozen years ago that we planted two apple trees, mail-ordered from Ohio. Because space was at a premium, we chose dwarf trees, but I no longer remember what varieties. One tree perished rather quickly—it was too close to first base.

The second tree seemed doomed from the start. It was grossly misshapen when it arrived, its trunk suffering from curvature of the spine—most trees resemble a T; this one looked like a C. It had only three or four spindly branches, and they were all on the same side, adding to the lopsidedness. I remember wondering whether I should plant the thing at an angle. That sapling was to apple trees what Charlie Brown's tiny pine is to Christmas trees.

Yet, year after year, I babied that tree. I pruned and shaped those limbs, and felt delight when new nubs turned into branches on the "bad side." I sprayed repeatedly. I wrapped the trunk with sticky tape each spring during gypsy-moth time, and daily inspected the tree almost leaf by leaf, picking off whatever caterpillars had climbed that high. All for a tree that produced nothing.

I don't know why I bothered; I'm not usually that patient. But something about that tree appealed to me. Maybe because it was so pathetic my tendency to root for the underdog came forward. After all, I still follow the Cleveland Indians.

The tree grew slowly, but it did grow, and gradually the shape improved, though it still won't win any prizes. The first blossoms appeared about four years ago—and were quickly frozen. I'm not sure what happened the last couple of years, but there have been no apples. Not one.

This year's blossom show was glorious—at least two dozen flowers—but I had no illusions. I had been burned too often. Only when the first apples actually appeared did I start thinking that this might be the year. I counted them: 11 apples. A bumper crop.

Then, when the apples were only slightly larger than marbles, they fell off—just dropped to the ground, two or three a day. Until only two remained. I kept expecting them to go, too, but they hung on, and now they are almost ripe. Both are getting redder almost by the hour. Any day now, they'll be ready.

We long ago decided that Bettie would get to eat one and I the other. The kids didn't get to vote. They can plant their own trees; they have more years ahead. Bettie even said she'd give me first choice. So for the past couple of weeks I've been sizing up those two apples, trying to decide which one I want. When you wait a dozen years for an apple, you want to be sure you get the right one.

Right now, both look good. In fact, they're perfect—probably the two finest apples this hillside has ever grown. But I can't shake the feeling that one is going to acquire a worm at the last minute. And I have no doubts at all who will get that apple.

46

First Frost

THE FIRST THING I notice is the silence. I don't even have to step outside to know something is different. No insects rasping. No birds twittering. No jays or crows squabbling. Even the robins and mockingbirds that began calling before dawn all summer are quiet. First frost is here.

Of course I knew this day was coming. Summer is gone, no matter what the calendar says. The calendar usually lags behind the seasons. It is now autumn. But until this particular morning, until first frost, it doesn't sink in. Now it's real.

So I go out early. I go out to greet the new season, to feel the difference, to experience a bit of magic. And first frost is magical. If it's a heavy frost—a "killing" frost, to gardeners—there is much to see in those precious moments of dawn and sunrise. By midmorning the frost will have vanished, too fragile for the glare of daylight.

Over the years, without really trying to, I've developed a route for my first-frost walk. It may vary a little, but not much, because it includes all the nearby places that present special scenes when touched with frost.

First stop, always, is the garden. The tomatoes are my gauge of how heavy the frost was. If the leaves are merely curled, I consider the frost light, and know the "best" frost will be in the hollows and low meadows, and will have to be felt as much as seen. However, if the tomato leaves and vines are limp and blackened, I know this is a big one. The gardening season is over, but there are compensations—the open fields and leaf-strewn paths and stream banks will be decorated with icy crystals that shimmer when touched by the sunshine. To me, it's a fair trade. I'd give up the last few tomatoes for magical scenes any time.

Just beyond the garden is a low, stony meadow. Eyes to the ground, I cross it slowly. Blackberry vines sprawl through the sparse grass, and when the frost is right, each blackberry leaf is transformed into a thing of delicate beauty. Already tinged with crimson or scarlet, the leaves are now fringed with exquisite silver ice particles. I can never resist picking a leaf or two and holding one up to the sky, toward the sunlight that has not yet reached the meadow. The effect is spectacular, but usually the

frost is so fragile, so delicate, that many of the fringes shatter upon the slightest movement or instantly melt from the warmth of my fingers.

Near the woods, I stoop to check the maple leaves that have already fallen and blown into the field. Like the blackberry leaves, they are outlined in silver, and at this moment they are more beautiful than any of the orange or golden leaves still on the trees. Each time I find such leaves I want to take them back to the house and show the family, but obviously that cannot be done. The frost would not survive the walk, much less a minute inside a warm house.

In a small wood lot, which I must pass through to reach the stream, it's as if there had been no frost; the trees keep the frost from reaching the path. I barely pause—I have to be at the water when the sunshine arrives.

A wispy mist is rising from the stream, a soft fog cloud that will shudder when the sun hits it, then glow brightly before starting to dissipate. The glow may last for only an instant, and I want to be there when it happens.

There is more to see at the stream, and I hurry to take in as much as possible. A spider web, bejeweled and sparkling. A goldenrod plume, gleaming as if truly gold. The open grassy area, winking in the sunshine as if somebody had scattered diamonds over it. I have to hurry; in minutes the grass, now sheathed in a film of ice, will be merely wet. The crystalline gems on the spider web will be drops of water. By midmorning, the goldenrod may look gray and bowed, aged and defeated.

I know there will be more warm days, more afternoons that feel like August instead of September. But right now, this morning, I can feel the shift of the seasons, I can feel autumn take hold. And right now, while the magic lasts, there is no place I would rather be. So I wander. I look. I linger. I don't want to leave.

47

Chipmunk Days

THESE ARE CHIPMUNK DAYS. It is a time of plenty in the woods, a time to prepare for winter, and for the chipmunk that means nonstop hurrying, nonstop hoarding.

Chipmunks aren't alone in gathering autumn's bounty, of course. Ants and bees, squirrels and woodchucks, muskrats and beavers; they're all working too, collecting now for the lean days far ahead. But it's hard to imagine any other creatures working with the energy and enthusiasm of the chipmunks.

Any wood lot worthy of the name has its population of chipmunks, particularly if there are oak trees and stone walls. Oak trees mean acorns, a major part of chipmunk diets, and stone walls mean safe places for dens. In fact, so many chipmunks live in and under stone walls, it's hard to imagine what the chipmunks did before the walls were built. Maybe they built their own rock piles.

There are so many oaks in southern New England forests that chipmunks would have an easy time if they did nothing but pick up acorns lying on the ground. But chipmunks don't necessarily do things the easy way; there wouldn't be any fun, any challenge, in simply scooping up acorns. Let squirrels do that. No, chipmunks prefer risking life and limb. Excitement and adventure seem as important to the chips as food.

I remember once pausing beneath an oak and watching a determined chipmunk that was dangling from a branch while attempting to pluck an acorn off a twig. The ground at my feet was littered with acorns—all apparently just as good as those still on the tree—but the chipmunk worked for many minutes, acrobatically clinging to the branch with its hind legs

while stretching for that one special acorn. When it finally chewed the acorn free, the chipmunk lost its balance for a moment and I put out my hands to catch it, so sure was I that it would fall; but it deftly secured a new hold, then scampered down the trunk. Almost at my feet, it searched through the fallen leaves and dozens of other acorns for its prize, stuffed it into its cheek pouch and dashed into a hole beneath the nearest stone wall.

It was obvious the chipmunk hadn't noticed me, or didn't care, so I stood still and waited. In a moment, it was back—again climbing the tree, again going through all kinds of contortions as it grappled with another virtually inaccessible acorn. When this one dropped, I stepped on it, just to see the chipmunk's reaction. It noticed my movement before descending the tree and went into a rage, flipping its tail with each scream as it cussed me out. For a full five minutes it ranted, its entire body shaking, sometimes stamping its feet with such righteous indignation that I nearly laughed out loud. Then it finally left the tree and circled around me to the stone wall. Still, it didn't depart until giving me one last piece of its mind.

Well, maybe the chipmunks and I are even now. There was an earlier chipmunk that had bugged me a bit. We had started stocking the bird feeder in October, as we usually do, and this chipmunk appeared almost immediately, arriving before the chickadees and house finches. It was apparently addicted to sunflower seeds, cramming half a dozen into its pouches, racing off, then returning in a few moments to steal another load.

At first, I didn't mind. Chipmunks are delightful to watch—most of the time—and I figured it wouldn't be long before this one curled up and went into hibernation. Let him have a few seeds for a midwinter snack. But days went by, then weeks. October slipped into November. Golden autumn faded into the bleakness of early winter. By the first snow, the chipmunk was still making its raids. What was this one, an insomniac? Aren't chipmunks supposed to sleep through winter?

I had found its den entrance, a tiny hole under the corner of the garage, and decided to take a look. It took a couple of hours of digging, but I eventually uncovered the tunnel, then its storage rooms. Inside were my sunflower seeds—perhaps a bushel of them. My first inclination was to retrieve them, but that didn't seem quite right. Winter was closing in; the chipmunk would need some food when he woke. I grumbled something about "just this one time" and reburied his loot.

By the next autumn, I had redesigned the feeder in an attempt to make it chipmunk-proof, but the thief never reappeared. Maybe the dog or a passing hawk had gotten it. Maybe it had stayed awake so long that it had to sleep through the whole next year. Maybe it had just decided that sunflower seeds were too easy and moved on to more exciting challenges.

Last year a chipmunk showed up occasionally in a meadow beyond the garden. This one sometimes seemed to think it was a junior-sized lion, and would stalk a cricket or grasshopper as a lion would stalk a gazelle. I never saw it catch an insect, so I don't know if it would have eaten one, but it was probably just having fun. That's the chipmunks' way. I've seen them climb weed stalks and then ride them to the ground, as my kids used to do with saplings. Once the weed stalks were down, the chipmunks would snip off the seed capsules and carry them off, but I often thought there were plenty of more accessible weed seeds available. That would be too easy, like picking up acorns.

No, they would rather make their food-gathering a fun event. At this time of year, the whole world is their playground and they intend to enjoy it. The instinct telling them to do things the harder but more adventurous ways is as strong as the instinct that demands that they store up goodies for the winter.

So they have hit upon an ideal combination; food and fun. And woe be to anything that interferes. Even humans.

48

The Numbers

THE NUMBERS CAN get to you. They can be staggering, overwhelming, beyond comprehension. In some ways, I suppose, the numbers can even be frightening, but they also can be most reassuring.

Autumn is when the sheer numbers of the natural world are most evident. How many acorns are littering the forest floor right now? How many goldenrods are blooming along the roadsides? How many red-winged blackbirds and swallows are in the flocks moving south? How many milkweed and thistle seeds are riding the wind? If you really want numbers, try figuring out how many leaves will be falling from just one maple, never mind a whole grove.

This is the time of dispersal. This is the time when the production of spring and summer, the bounty of the year, is scattered to prepare for another spring and another growing season. That way, replacements are always ready and waiting. It's not a bad system at all.

But wander around the countryside right now, and take a look at what's out there. It seems every tree, every plant, has gone overboard. If only a small fraction of those acorns sprouted, we'd have the densest oak forest in our history. If one-hundredth of the thistle seeds, or the milkweed seeds, took root, they'd fill up every inch of yard and field and pasture. A naturalist once counted the seeds in a single goldenrod plume, and came up with more than 15,000; can you imagine what New England would look like if there were 15,000 times more goldenrods next year than this year?

Obviously, that never happens. The vast majority of seeds won't sprout. A great many are eaten by birds and animals. Far more simply do not find suitable soil. Too dry. Too wet. Too stony. Too sandy. Too much acidity. Too little acidity. Too much shade. Too much sunshine.

So the vast numbers are necessary. No matter how it may look, we're not going to have our lawns covered over by goldenrods. Most of the seeds never have a chance. But enough will take hold that we can expect another display of the golden plumes next fall, for better or worse.

How the seeds are scattered can be as fascinating as the numbers. Acorns, of course, are too heavy to be carried by the wind. Most simply fall from the oaks and lie on the forest floor. Those have little chance of sprouting. But a few may roll from beneath the parent tree and find enough room and sunshine. Squirrels and chipmunks and jays will carry off some of the others, often dropping or burying as many as they eat. Perhaps half a dozen of the thousands of acorns falling from one large oak will sprout, and if just one of those sprouts survives to adulthood, the continuation of the species will be assured.

Maple seeds wander farther. Because each seed is equipped with a wing, it whirls on its downward flight, like an out-of-control helicopter, instead of falling straight down. With a gust of wind, it can land some distance from the parent tree.

The wind is the distributor of many plant seeds. You can see it almost every day now. Milkweeds and thistles and the late dandelions and so many others. The seeds are contained in the tiny, fluffy bits of fiber that are carried by even the slightest breezes. They ride along, like miniature parachutes, until dropping lightly to earth.

Birds scatter seeds, too. Most of the wild fruits—raspberries, elderberries, blueberries, grapes, cherries—are planted with seeds that pass through the birds' bodies after they've consumed the berries. Multiflora roses and viburnums and pokeweeds and numerous less desirable plants are scattered the same way.

People who wander the fields in fall, or have dogs that do, have to be familiar with another form of seed dispersal—hitchhiking. Each fall when Rusty and I get back from our walks, we have to spend a half-hour pulling out all the burs and sticktights that we've unintentionally collected, he on his tail and legs, me on my socks and pants legs and shoelaces.

Sometimes, as I sit there and try to extract the burs, I grumble about how many there are, and ask if it's really necessary for those plants to produce such a number. But I know the answer. They have a job to do, the same as the acorns and the maple seeds and the silky milkweed floss. To make sure next spring is green. To continue the cycle. They do their jobs well.

Autumn

49

The Hearth

Some years, we don't even wait until the first frost. All it takes is one drizzly or raw day, and we're ready to light a fire. That first evening at the hearth is special.

Yes, fireplaces are inefficient and, yes, they waste heat and, yes, they can be dirty, but we would not be without one. Especially now, when the season's first chills are beginning to creep in. This is fireside time.

A fireplace is probably more important now than in midwinter. Then, it's too cold for the fireplace to do much good; we have to rely on the furnace. But now, when just a bit of warmth is needed, as much for the soul as for the body, the hearth fire is just about perfect.

Once the first fire of autumn is lit, the rest of the family drifts into the room, one by one. Perhaps it's the crackling flames that draw them, or the simmering hiss, or maybe the pungent aroma of the smoke. Whatever it is, they crowd around, some poking the embers and adding sticks and logs, others just watching the flames dance.

This fascination with fireplaces is a little incongruous. Fireplaces are left over from the time when homes had hand-dug wells and kerosene lamps. And don't forget the outdoor privies. I don't know of anybody who regrets their passing.

Now, we insist on central air conditioning, several bathrooms, telephones in every room, home computers and gadgets to record the television shows we might miss.

And we still want a fireplace.

Why? Well, not just to warm our hands, that's for sure. Any kind of furnace or stove heats better than a fireplace. No, it's more than that.

We find comfort in an open fire. Psychologists theorize the need for a fire is our link to ancestors back to cave men, who first tamed fire and learned to bask in the safety of the glow while wolves prowled the darkness.

Whether that is right or not, I don't know. Nor does it matter very much. I know only that I like fires.

When I worked a job that gave me afternoon hours at home alone, I looked forward to an occasional rainy day almost as much as I delighted

in October's crisp, sunny days, when the dog and I roamed through the woods and fields. When it rained, we moved indoors, Rusty snoozing at my side and I in a comfortable chair, my feet on the hearth, losing myself in books.

The writings of John Muir, John Burroughs and Henry David Thoreau are particularly appropriate for fireside reading, as are the books of 20th century naturalists such as Aldo Leopold, Hal Borland and Edwin Way Teale. I often read Jack London's tales of the Yukon a little later, when the snow is flying and the winter wind is howling. London's books really make you appreciate a glowing fire.

There was no fireplace in our house when we moved in, but we had one in our previous home and missed it dearly. After a few years without one, we decided we just couldn't last through any more New England winters unless we could return to the hearth.

Having one built proved interesting. We wanted a big one, taking up half a wall, and only fieldstone would do. The mason we hired—a craftsman in every sense of the word—spoke almost no English, and we cannot speak Italian. He lugged a truckload of stones of every shape into the room, covering the floor, and proceeded to create a work of art, choosing them with an expert eye and fitting them together like a giant jigsaw puzzle.

That was before the boom in wood-stove heating, and for a while we considered converting the fireplace, but we just couldn't do it.

A stove would heat better, of course, and the manufacturers of stoves have wisely made many with glass fronts so the flames can be seen, but it's still not the same. Not to us.

All is in readiness now. There are a couple of cords of wood stacked in the backyard. There is enough wood, dry and seasoned, in the basement for the first several fires. I've chopped plenty of kindling. And there are quite a few books that I've been saving for a special time. For now, for fireside time.

50

Tipsy Robins

Most songbirds are already heading south, or soon will be, but not those on Pokeweed Hill. They're enjoying themselves too much.

Maybe they are better off not trying to fly right now anyway. They're a little tipsy.

Pokeweeds produce blackish, juicy berries that a great many birds find irresistible—especially the robins—and it seems the berries are more plentiful than usual this year. As long as the supply holds out, the robins are likely to hang around.

However, the fruit can be a little intoxicating to birds that consume large amounts, particularly late in the season.

Right now, the pokeweed is one of the more easily noticed plants around the countryside. It's big, up to ten feet tall, and its stalks are a brilliant red-pink. And they're laden with those clusters of purple-black berries, of course.

John Burroughs, in *A Bunch of Herbs* (1881), wrote, "Pokeweed is a native American, and what a lusty, royal plant it is! It never invades cultivated fields, but hovers about the borders and looks over the fences like a painted Indian sachem. Thoreau coveted its strong purple stalk for a cane."

I'm not sure it is quite that admirable, but it is an interesting plant in more ways than its effect on birds. It has several regional names—inkberry, pigeonberry, pokeberry, scoke—and each hints of the weed's past as well as its present.

Anybody who has crushed a pokeweed berry knows where the inkberry name comes from. The thick, crimson juice really does look

like ink. It is said that a great many letters sent home from the field during the Civil War were written with pokeweed juice. Some of those letters are still legible.

Indians used the juice as a dye of sorts—poke comes from an Indian word pokan, which means stain or dye—and early Colonists tried it but found the colors faded quickly when applied to wool and linen.

Pigeonberry refers to the way vast flocks of passenger pigeons swarmed down and stuffed themselves with the berries each October. This may explain why there are no more passenger pigeons.

The roots, as well as the seeds, are poisonous to people, but in some places the tender sprouts of spring are sought as "greens" and eaten like asparagus. Also, there was a time when parts of the plant were used in poultices and home remedies.

The plants spread quickly—mostly because birds scatter the seeds in their droppings—and seem to be about the first to take hold in new ground. That's the way it was with Pokeweed Hill.

Several years ago, a mound of topsoil was pushed aside by bulldozers seeking the sand and gravel beneath, and an instant hill was formed. In a matter of months, pokeweeds were growing all over it, and the stand gets thicker each year.

The weeds gave us some anxious moments when our daughters were young. I found them playing in the backyard one day "making pies" of the "pretty berries." We became frantic, even though they assured us they had not eaten any. As it turned out, they hadn't, but I still went out and chopped down all the stalks within a hundred yards. Not that it did much good; they come right back up every spring.

The bird that relies most heavily on the pokeberries is the mourning dove, a distant cousin of the old passenger pigeon, but on Pokeweed Hill I see a dozen robins for every dove. There are catbirds and jays there, too, and cedar waxwings and mockingbirds, and sometimes a cardinal or two, but robins outnumber all the others combined.

I've read reports of birds staggering and being unable to fly after a pokeberry binge, but I've never seen any reach that stage. Even so, the robins seem to be enjoying themselves back there. They chirp and squeal and holler to each other as they gulp down a few berries, fly to the nearby maples and then hurry right back. Maybe they're checking to be sure they still can fly.

It won't be long now until the bar will be closed—er, the berries will be gone—and then the robins will be pulling out once more. Then this strange but "lusty, royal plant" will fade into the background again until late next summer. I'm sure the robins will be waiting.

51

Lure of the Night

SOMETIMES, THE OWL is the excuse. Sometimes, it's the geese, or the fox that I say I want to find. Most of the time, though, it is the night itself that draws me to the hillside. The night and the moon.

Autumn nights are special. Both crisp and soft, both soothing and exhilarating. Walking familiar paths becomes an enchanting new experience after darkness falls and the moon climbs high. To those who have gone to the woods at night, the moon's lure becomes virtually irresistible. The call is loud and clear; it should be answered.

The full moons of autumn seem fuller, larger, nearer than the moons of summer. More golden, too. They bathe the countryside in a glowing light that makes flashlights unnecessary, even in the forest. In fact, artificial lights seem out of place, intrusive, on such nights.

In the old days, September's moon was called the harvest moon, and that of October the hunter's moon. Both names were appropriate for decades but now are outdated, at least in this part of the country. When harvesting was done by hand—cutting corn, shocking corn, husking corn—farmers needed to work all the hours they could. That meant returning to the fields after supper and the evening milking. As bright as autumn moons are, a farmer could easily shock or cut corn without lanterns.

Then, when the work was finished, it was time to enjoy the nights, and countrymen turned to sport, using the moonlight for raccoon hunts. The night would ring with the baying of prized coonhounds on the trail. The hunts became social events of a sort, as the men often gathered around campfires, bragging about their dogs and swapping lies while they waited for the dogs to tree a coon. It was a means of having some fun while reducing the number of raccoons, which can be major headaches to farmers.

Modern machinery harvests corn so rapidly there is no longer a need to work after dark, and there are far fewer coon hunters in these parts now. But the nights have not changed. They are still too precious to be wasted sitting in front of a television.

So I go out walking. Usually to the rocky hillside. If I'm lucky, I hear a great horned owl hooting up there—as I did just a few nights ago—and if I'm very, very lucky, I catch a glimpse of the big owl as it swoops over a mouse-infested meadow. One of the most memorable sights I've ever had was watching the owl sail by, on soundless wings, within 15 feet of me on a night so bright I could see its yellow eyes burning through the half-darkness and its deadly talons gleaming in the moonlight. I haven't seen the owl since, but I keep looking.

It's almost the same with the fox. I know there is at least one up on the ridge. I've heard it yipping a few times, and its tracks are common throughout the winter, but seeing it is another matter. Once, as I stepped from the woods into a clearing near the ridge, I thought I saw it. Just a flash, a blur. Maybe it was only my imagination; I'm not sure. Maybe this fall I can get a better look.

I don't know how many times I've walked the October nights hoping to see a flock of migrating geese pass overhead, silhouetted against the moon. It's a scene that has been painted thousands of times by thousands of artists—it seems to be a requirement for nature painters—but I've never seen it myself. I've heard flocks crossing the sky in the darkness, and I've seen many geese at other times of the day, but I've yet to see the legendary wanderers pass in front of the moon. So I keep looking.

In reality though, geese and foxes and owls aren't necessary to make the night walks intriguing. They are only fringe benefits, bonuses. More dependable are the long shadows over the paths, the faint whispers in the hemlocks, the silvery gleam on the pond, the rustle of something—you're never quite sure what—scurrying through the fallen leaves. Often, there is the winey fragrance of wild grapes, and perhaps the poignancy of wood smoke. If you are near an orchard, there is the aroma of apples, a particularly heady smell if there has been a frost. If the temperature is sufficiently cool, there is the crispness of the night air, and the soft glow of your own breath clouds.

Night walking is not for the chatterboxes, or those in a hurry. Go quietly and slowly. Stop often. Tune in all your senses. Soak up the sounds and the smells and the feelings, as well as the sights. Chances are you'll come back with your blood pressure a bit lower and your contentment a shade higher.

And it might be just as well if you don't see an owl or fox or flock of geese. Then, you'll have a good excuse for going out there again tomorrow night.

52

My Own Migration Flight

EVERY FALL I feel this way. I see the flocks of birds gathering for migration—the swallows and flickers, the redwings and warblers—and I get envious. I want to go, too. Hey, wait for me!

It's not that I yearn to spend winter in the Gulf States or Central America. Quite the contrary; I enjoy snow and ice— up to a point, of course. It's just that the birds' freedom to wander at will is so appealing. I want to do that. October makes me yearn to go roaming. For me, it's the call of the wild.

New England has done this to me.

Before I came to New England, October meant the World Series and football games, picking corn and starting the fall plowing. The season was pleasant but hectic, the foliage was pretty but not spectacular. Not like New England's.

Now October means awesome foliage, but far more than that, too. It's cloudless mornings and hazy evenings, stirring breezes and perfect temperatures. It's the poignant aromas of ripe apples and ready grapes, the alluring sounds of geese overhead and foxes yipping in the night.

Put it all together, and it means wanderlust. It makes me want to keep moving, to see more. What's over the next hill? Around the bend in the river? Farther down the beach? That's why I want to join the birds; they get to see it all.

If I were to join a specific flock of birds, I think I'd choose the flickers. Swallows leave too early. Warblers fly at night too much, and have to work too hard, going such long distances on such tiny wings. Geese fly in those neat V-formations, but they fly so high and go so far between rests I don't think they see much of the countryside. And they get shot at a lot.

Flickers seem to have the right idea. For those unfamiliar with flickers, they're big, rather eccentric woodpeckers that spend more time on the ground, eating ants, than in trees. They're all business during nesting time, but once that is out of the way they take it easy. They start flocking in August and spend a month or two just wandering around, carefree as the breeze, aimless as the wind-blown leaves. My kind of way of spending October.

Still, I don't think I'd restrict myself to the flickers. Some of the other birds go places that the flickers do not, and at this time of year I want it all.

Most of the birds funnel down to the coast, then follow the shoreline south. That's not a bad idea, but I would join them for only part of the journey. I'd spend a couple of days flying around Block Island, a resting place for hundreds and hundreds of migrants—both land and water birds—each October. It's simply delightful out there right now. Sunshine. Invigorating breezes. Few people.

The South County (for non-Rhode Islanders, "South County" is Washington County, the southernmost of the state's five) beaches and Cape Cod would draw me for similar reasons. I seldom visit those places in summer, because traffic jams, gasoline fumes, burning sand and blaring radios are not my idea of fun. But in October, when there are miles of open shores and the loudest noises are the wind and the waves, I want to be there, wheeling with the gulls, strolling with the sandpipers. Napatree Point and Ninigret are great beaches for dallying in fall, and the Cape's National Seashore may be even better. It's certainly bigger.

But I'd reverse the birds' routes, too, and go north and west. I'd wander through the small villages on the Maine coast now that the tourists are gone. I'd paddle around the clear, cold inland ponds with the loons. I'd soar above the majestic White Mountains with the ravens, and float down the streams with the mergansers. I'd glide through every farming valley in Vermont, cherishing the silence of frosty mornings and the bounty of harvest. I'd linger in the Berkshires, riding the wind with the hawks, until the maples' golds and oranges had faded and withered.

By then, October will be ending, and the sharpness of November will be in the air. The other birds will be at their winter quarters, so maybe I, too, will be ready to settle in, with fireplace crackling and feet on the hearth.

But until then, let's fly.

53

Hornets and Mixed Feelings

THE HORNET NEST is deserted now. I can take it apart and examine it at my leisure. No hurry. No worry. No stings. The hornets' days are gone. I've outlived one more colony of them.

For all the things that we like to lump together as "bugs", there are only two seasons. One is filled with frantic activity, the other is months of dormancy. Individual lives are quickly spent—often going through hatching, growth, mating and death in a day or two—but the species go on. When frost comes, such cold-blooded creatures can no longer function and they vanish. However, they have already made arrangements for returning next spring.

It isn't only the bugs. Frogs and toads, turtles and salamanders, snakes and lizards quietly steal away, too. They bury themselves in mud or burrow beneath rocks or logs, curling up in some refuge where instinct tells them the cold won't reach.

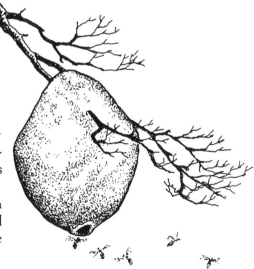

I think about such things now, as the cold weather approaches: the ingenuity of the insects and reptiles and other lower animals to survive, to ensure their futures. With some of the bugs, I'm not sure I like the idea. I probably wouldn't miss the mosquitoes if they failed to show up next spring; I could live without blackflies and gnats and ticks, too. And I have mixed feelings about the hornets.

At this time of year, when most of the leaves are down, I find many

hornet nests. Big gray, roundish structures, the nests are often attached to branches of bushes. They're endlessly intriguing, with their papery coverings, ventilation systems and intricate layers of hexagonal cells. I'm impressed all over again each fall when I realize that these elaborate nests, often the size of basketballs, were built in one summer by a bunch of insects.

But I'm glad I didn't find these nests earlier in the year, when the tough, eager-to-sting hornets were still active. For me, no other New England insect has a sting quite as painful. Not the wasp or yellowjacket, not the honeybee or bumblebee—those, I more or less ignore. Hornets, however, especially the white-headed variety that scientists call bald-faced hornets, have my respect. I don't mind waiting until fall to examine their nests.

Of course, there are a few times every summer when we cross paths unintentionally. It happens most often when I'm picking wild raspberries or blueberries. I'll be happily gathering the berries when I reach into a leafy bush and get zapped. Instantly, my arm will feel as though it's on fire. I jump back and see how fast I can get away. And that's with just one sting; a multiple attack can bring screams.

Most of the time, though, we coexist rather peacefully. When I find a nest, I let it be. And each fall I find nests in places I've been around all summer without realizing the baldies were that close—so, clearly, they aren't always out looking for trouble.

This year, however, was a bit different. Way back in early spring, probably shortly after the hornet queen had emerged from her hibernation, I noticed a nest being built under the eaves of our garden shed. That was okay; I figured it would be interesting to watch the colony develop. I warned my family, overriding the votes for eviction, and cautiously welcomed our new neighbors.

The colony thrived without incident and was nearly forgotten until a day in mid-July when I was ambushed. I was minding my own business working in the garden, at least 50 feet from the shed, when one of them hit without warning. It was a sneak attack, a sting right in the middle of my back. I never saw the culprit, but I knew it was one of the hornets. Nothing else stings like that.

Ungrateful wretches! I had let them have free room and board and this was how they repaid me! Too angry for common sense, I marched to the shed ready for a fight—and found an abandoned nest. It was undamaged, and many of the cells still held unhatched eggs, but every hornet was gone. They had left, for reasons I still haven't figured out. Not knowing where they had relocated but fairly certain it was somewhere near the garden made us a little leery about spending much time out there the rest of the summer. It was a good excuse for letting the weeds go.

There were no more attacks, and eventually I found the nest, almost touching the ground under a bush beyond the garden fence. This one, too, is empty now. As always, frost has wiped out the colony, ending the hornets' brief but frenzied lives.

Except for the new queens. These few females survive, hiding somewhere in crevices or below ground, hibernating. They will go through the winter with only the faintest flicker of life still in their bodies, but they are carrying the future generations. They're just waiting for the signal to start.

It's rather incredible, something worth thinking about as cold weather approaches. I just hope these queens wake up next spring in somebody else's backyard.

54

October Osprey

First it's a scream off in the distance. That's what I have been waiting for. Several moments later, there are wings flashing in the fading sunshine. Then, those fierce, defiant eyes. Staring. Glaring. Daring.

My watch has paid off. The osprey is back.

At this time of year, many people interested in birds of prey gather on tops of mountains or at strategic points along the ocean for the hawk migration. They are disappointed if they cannot count birds by the hundreds. I'm satisfied with one bird, this osprey.

In what is becoming a ritual of autumn, an osprey has returned to an inland pond in the northern part of the state where I live. For four years in a row, an osprey—I wish I knew whether it's the same bird—has stopped by in October. It spends a few weeks there, then disappears.

There is little doubt that the big fish hawk is merely dallying at the pond, resting a bit, on its fall migration south. Maybe it nests in Maine or even farther up the coast, and the pond is the end of the first leg of its annual journey. But I keep hoping it is more than that.

Each fall when the osprey arrives, I wonder whether it is considering the pond for a new home. It spends much of its time in the sheltered coves, perching in the highest trees, as if checking out possible nesting sites. That may not be the case at all—it probably isn't—but I'd like to think it is.

There are few birds that I find more impressive. Ospreys have style. Their appearance is sharp: basically white with black face markings that look something like masks. They have dark backs and their wings are dark above and white below, resplendent in sunshine. I go looking for

"my" osprey in early evening, at a time when the slanting sunshine catches the bird's undersides and sets it gleaming. Against a hillside backdrop of autumn-colored leaves, the sight is something to behold.

On top of that, an osprey's lifestyle is as appealing as its looks. It's a graceful flier and expert fisherman, plunging out of the sky into water and snaring fish with powerful talons. Its scream in flight is the sound of wildness itself, as untamable as that penetrating stare of its yellow eyes. It seems to regard humans as the enemy, and I guess it has good reason.

Ospreys have been increasing slowly over the past several years, but so far none nest in my part of the state. State wildlife officials say that 23 nests were found in Rhode Island this year, most of them along the coast and in the Great Swamp. Now 23 may not sound like a lot of nests, considering that several hundred ospreys once lived on Narragansett Bay and along the South County shoreline. But 20 years ago there were only two or three nests in the state, and the osprey was in danger of dying out altogether in southern New England.

Most of the blame for the birds' decline has been put on DDT and other chemicals used extensively in the 1950s and '60s. The chemicals found their way into the water, where they were ingested by the fish. Ospreys ate the fish, and though the poison didn't often kill the birds outright, it created a disaster with the eggs. Often, the eggs had no shells at all, or shells so thin they collapsed as soon as the parent birds attempted to sit on them. Other eggs simply would not hatch; the birds might as well have been laying rocks.

There were other factors in the ospreys' decline, too. The surge in building along the Bay and the saltwater ponds crowded birds out. Ospreys need room, and they don't particularly like people. Also, there were fewer and fewer large dead trees left standing. Where were the birds to build their bulky stick nests?

Eventually, DDT was banned, and even though it took a long time, ospreys gradually began rebuilding their numbers. After it was discovered that they like putting their nests atop high poles—usually electrical poles, away from trees—some people started helping out. Poles with platforms on top were put up near potential osprey areas, places that had plenty of fish and little human disturbance. It was a wise move, and now the great majority of osprey nests in Rhode Island are on these platformed poles.

Perhaps that would be the answer for keeping the osprey coming to the pond in my area. Maybe a pole at the right place, like out on a point or on an island, would convince the bird that this is a good place to live, as well as a great place to visit.

Of course, it takes two ospreys for a nest, and I've yet to see this bird's mate along on these October interludes. Maybe they split up so that both can look for new neighborhoods. Maybe they simply take separate migration routes, the way some married couples take separate vacations.

At any rate, one osprey is back again this year, and that is important indeed. It would be great if the bird became a permanent resident, but just seeing it dive for fish and listening to its cry are more than a little satisfying. It is reason to be grateful that such splendid birds were not wiped out altogether, and it is reason to make sure that their future is made brighter.

55

Return of the Chestnut

THE ANTICIPATION—and the apprehension—increases as I near the spot. I haven't expected that. After all, it's only a tree I'm going to see.

Well, maybe I shouldn't say it's only a tree. It is a chestnut, and chestnuts should never be taken lightly. There just aren't enough of them these days. That's why I'm apprehensive; I'm never sure when I stop by whether this tree will still be alive. How long can it last before the infamous blight finds it?

At the stone wall, I leave the path. Let's see, I think it's only about 20 yards in, near the clearing.

Hey, there it is! Still looking healthy and hearty, thank goodness. The tree has the distinctive long, sharply toothed leaves that are golden brown at this time of year. It even has a few clusters of the spine-covered seed capsules—containing the kind of nut that our ancestors supposedly roasted over open fires—and where there are seeds, there has to be some optimism for the future.

Still, there's no sense of triumph. Not yet. Just a feeling of relief. It's far too soon to get excited. The tree has merely survived one more year; it has taken one more step on the perilous road to maturity, but it still has a long way to go. Right now, it is only about six inches in diameter and maybe 25 feet tall.

But I've never seen a full-grown American chestnut growing wild, so this tree is important to me. Chances are this one won't make it, either—but as long as there is life, there is hope.

Chestnuts once were the dominant trees of New England forests. In dense stands, they grew tall and straight. In open areas, they spread out, the crowns reaching 80, 90, 100 feet across. Great trees, spectacular trees, or so say the old-timers and the history books.

It's been about 80 years since the blight came. Apparently, infected trees from Asia were brought to New York City, and once the fungus reached this country, it spread rapidly. Insects, birds and the wind dispersed the spores. In a few decades, virtually all the chestnuts were dead or dying.

By the time foresters were aware of what was happening, it was too late. Since then, there have been great efforts to bring back the trees—all without success. Most of the emphasis lately has been on crossing the American chestnut with the Chinese and Japanese varieties, which are more resistant to the blight. I suppose a hybrid chestnut is better than no chestnut, but it would be so much better if the native tree, the authentic American chestnut, were once more to shade our hillsides.

For years after the great trees had died, their skeletons stood in the woods—silent, stark, yet eloquent testimony to still another case of our destructive foolishness in taking something out of its natural environment. Think of it: starlings, house sparrows, the blankety-blank gypsy moths. There are dozens more examples.

Now, even most of the moldering stumps of the old chestnuts are gone. But the roots haven't given up. Year after year, new sprouts pop up from the roots, striving to replace the long-vanished giants. The saplings seem to thrive for a few years, but then they become infected and succumb the way the parent tree did.

But although it's a discouraging cycle, there are rays of hope. There seem to have been more clumps of the sprouts appearing in the last few years. Maybe the gypsy moths have even helped in that regard; by defoliating the oaks and so letting the sunshine in, maybe they are giving the chestnuts a new chance.

And it's possible that the blight is losing some of its punch after all these years. Maybe the chestnuts are finally building up some resistance of their own. Such things do happen occasionally.

So the story of the American chestnut is not quite finished. The ending is still in doubt. Each time I see that a sprout has progressed into a sapling, and each year I see that "my" tree has grown another few inches, I feel a little more hopeful. Don't count the chestnuts out yet.

56

Indian Summer

INDIAN SUMMER IS a special time. Always has been. But it's not quite the same now. I miss the corn shocks.

When we get a few days of unusually mild weather in late October or November, it's like being handed a bonus. It's another chance—perhaps the last chance—to do some of the things of summer before bracing for winter.

But I cannot think of Indian summer without thinking of corn shocks. Childhood images last a long time.

Just how or why this period of warm days and calm nights was named for Indians is open to speculation. Supposedly, the New England Indians of colonial times told their white neighbors to expect such a period, that there would be time to get in the corn and stock up on game and make other preparations for winter. Other versions of the name's derivation say that the Indians used these days for staging attacks, or that the haze that lingers on the horizon at this time of year was caused by Indian campfires.

I have no idea which story is right—maybe bits of all of them were combined over the years—but I do know where my own images of Indian summer originated. In the middle of a cornfield, in the middle of October, when I was about eight years old.

My father and brothers were cutting the corn, by hand, and building shocks. That's the way corn was handled in the days before mechanical pickers. The stalks were tied in bundles, and then a number of bundles were stacked upright and bound together with twine. These shocks, much wider at the base than at the top, were able to withstand winter weather, protecting the ears of corn until the farmers had time to do the husking. Unless, of course, the shocks were pushed over by Halloween pranksters.

It was evening when I joined my father and brothers. Darkness was settling in, a soft darkness that seemed to edge out from the nearby woods. Crickets were chirping. There was a faint rustling among the dry corn leaves, even though there didn't seem to be any wind blowing. A pumpkin-colored moon was rising.

As we walked back home, my father gazed over the fields, and said so softly I thought he was talking to himself, "Indian summer might be the best time of the year."

It must have been the first time I had heard that term, because I asked him what he meant. He smiled, put one hand on my shoulder and waved his other hand toward the shocks all around us. "Look at all the tepees we have out here," he said. "We've built our own Indian village."

The image stuck. For years afterward, even when I was out there building the shocks myself, I could see Indian villages in the cornfields.

Apparently, Dad and I weren't the only ones who had imagination. I was grown up and off the farm when I first saw a reproduction of a cartoon that once ran in a Chicago newspaper. It gave me chills; the people in it could have been Dad and me.

In the cartoon, drawn by a man named John T. McCutcheon, a man and boy are burning leaves next to a field of corn shocks. The man is telling the story of Indian summer, and as he talks the scene changes in the boy's eyes: Not only do the shocks turn into tepees, and the burning leaves become a campfire, but the blowing leaves suddenly are dancing Indian braves. The boy is captivated. I know just how he felt.

These days, it's hard to find corn shocks, so I'm not sure what images the term Indian summer conjures up for kids. It's not important, I suppose; no more important than exactly what constitutes Indian summer. That's another debate: Some people say it cannot occur before November; others say it's any warm spell after a killing frost.

None of it matters. Indian summer is too delightful to argue about. It's meant to be enjoyed, whether that means raking leaves or getting in one last fishing trip or wandering for miles over the hills. I try to do all of these things during Indian summer, but my mind is usually on a long-ago evening and corn shocks and a warm, gentle man.

57

The Season of November

THIS IS A NEW SEASON, one called November. It's an in-between time, an interval between October's spectacular colors and December's ice and snow. It's a time of transition: not quite winter, but no longer autumn. That's why I think of November as a season all by itself.

It's not a particularly popular month. Once they've mentioned Thanksgiving Day, most people seem to have a tough time finding anything else to look forward to now. But there can be more to this month than turkey and cranberry sauce.

November allows us to slow down after the flash and dash of October, to get back to fundamentals. When the fall foliage is at its finest, most of us have a tendency to hurry, to race from one ridge to another, even from one mountain to another, searching for more scenes to marvel at. It's fun and exciting, but too often all we do is ooh and aah for a moment, and perhaps snap a picture, and then we rush off to the next grove of maples.

Now, though, the flamboyance is gone, and so is the urgency. Now, instead of hurrying, we can stroll along in contemplation, relishing the more subtle colors of this season: bronze and copper, old gold and burnt orange, mahogany and tan. Together they give the countryside a mellow look, a richness that glows rather than explodes, soothes rather than inspires. The softening ambience affects my mood. I find myself walking more slowly, stopping more often, looking deeper, and perhaps even thinking more.

There is much to think about. When gowned in greenery, the forests and hills have a certain sameness, but with the foliage stripped away,

they gain a measure of individuality. Now I can see rocks and ridges and ravines that mark each hill's profile. The leafless trees provide "a concentration on the essential," as one writer put it. I like that phrase.

Now I can see past the trees to the essentials, the basic structure of the hillsides. I see the ancient ledges and marvel all over again at the fascinating formations left behind by the glaciers. Huge boulders—often as big as a house—were sliced like a pound of butter. Imagine the awesome might, the weight and strength, that the glaciers had to carry to do something like that.

In the opened-up scenery of November, I'm also drawn to the stone walls and cellar holes and long-forgotten woods roads. They, too, invite contemplation. Who built them? What was life like back then? Why did these people choose this site, and why did they leave? I'm repeatedly struck by two wonders: that anybody worked as hard as those old-timers did in building all those miles of walls, and that anybody could consider farming in such stony soil.

Apparently, the rocks eventually won out. The farmers gave up, either moving to less hostile land farther west, or shifting to other lines of work. It all happened long ago, but the efforts of those farmers remain in their legacies of stone. At times, I can still feel their presence.

So I dally in such places. I wander the old lanes, poke around in the cellar holes, follow the rambling walls. I try to locate the wells and the barn foundations. And quite often I find myself spending time in the tiny graveyards, musing on lives lived out, mostly quietly and anonymously, where squirrels and grouse and foxes now reside.

This season, before snow hides them, is a good time for noticing tiny things that are always in the woods but that most of the year are overwhelmed. Gray-green lichens decorate the rocks. Patches of moss, soft as carpet, cling to the slopes and old trees. Lowly evergreen plants of many varieties—pipsissewa, plantain, partridgeberry, wintergreen—are scattered across the forest floor.

This is the season for looking around, for getting to know the land. Now, when we're not dazzled by showy foliage or closed out by curtains of leaves, we can gain a richer appreciation and a deeper understanding —maybe even come to a few satisfying conclusions.

On the other hand, we may find that instead of answers, we gather only more questions. But that is good, too. In November, we can concentrate on the essential.

58

Woods Work

EACH NOVEMBER I feel the pull all over again. For a few weeks, in this lull between autumn and winter, I fancy myself a woodsman. This is the time for working in the forest.

Usually, I take only an ax and a bow saw. Sometimes, my sons go along. Other times, my only companion is Rusty, the aging golden retriever. We seldom have more than an hour or two. Darkness comes too early now.

But I have to be out there. I'm adding a little more firewood to the stacks in the backyard, but that's only an excuse. Thanks to Hurricane Gloria, I already have enough firewood for not only this winter but probably the next one as well. Still, I wander off to the hillside whenever I get the chance.

This is a new season in the forest. The flamboyance of October is fading; the scarlets and red-oranges are already only memories. The woods are not yet bare, however; just different. There is a burnished look to the forest now. Bronze and old gold and burnt orange are the colors. They offer a warm, comforting glow, rather than the exciting displays of a couple of weeks ago. Now, instead of hurrying from one ridge to another, searching for more scenes to exclaim about, we can stroll in quiet contemplation. The softening hues reflect my feelings; there is no need to hurry now. Let's enjoy this extra season, this reprieve before cold rain and icy wind.

Instead of maples and dogwoods, it is time to notice the lesser lights. Like sassafras, as yellow as sunlight. And the ferns, unnoticed most of the year but now a rich golden brown that seems to hold the day's light as dusk settles over the woods.

On my hillside there are two kinds of trees that just now are coming to the forefront. One is an overlooked little tree whose name is shown in most books as half English and half Latin: maple-leafed viburnum. Nobody pays it any attention during the summer, but now it is lovely.

Not much larger than a bush, the viburnum has leaves shaped like those of the maple, but they change color much later. Right now, they are a deep red-purple. But they are meant to be touched, not just looked at. They are the softest leaves I know, almost like velvet, with a downy fuzz on the underside. These viburnums also produce tiny black berries, but it's the leaves that stop me.

The other shrub-tree of November is the witch hazel, which blooms when other plants are closing up for winter. It always looks out of place covered with clusters of yellow blossoms at a time when the forest floor is ankle-deep in dead leaves. Nobody seems to know for sure where the name originated —the plant is not related to hazelnuts —but somehow it fits. If the witches of Halloween ever want to dress up their black costumes, the twisted and curled blossoms of the witch hazel would be most appropriate.

Most of the trees on this hillside are oaks, and earlier in autumn I sometimes feel cheated that there aren't more of the maples and hickories and birches that give other forests their riotous colors. But now I am satisfied with the oaks. Nobody thinks of oak leaves as colorful, and they certainly can't compare with maples, but by November they reach a subtle, almost dignified range of colors. Russet. Mahogany. Maroon. Colors of strength; colors of substance. They assure us these aren't leaves that snap off in the first breeze. They'll be around most of the winter, rattling in the wind, standing up to the storms.

As I roam the woods, searching for fallen branches to chop and saw, I keep an eye out for other colors, and find plenty. Bittersweet, a woody vine that swarms over some trees, is displaying its orange berries. On the ground, among the dead leaves, are always-green partridgeberries, with their summery cherry-red fruit. Among the rocks on the ledges is the tiny red-capped lichen with the picturesque name British soldiers.

The woods are not winter-silent yet, either. As any woodsman knows, the minute he starts sawing, the chickadees gather round, adding their carefree twittering to his own noise. They welcome human visitors, and often will follow along as we travel from one part of the woods to another. There are other birds in the forest, too—the last of the robins and the first of the juncos— but it is the chickadees that we count on for company. They seem to take it upon themselves to assure us that even though the orioles and thrushes are gone, there will be friendly voices out there all winter.

I often linger on the hillside until the sun slips behind the opposite side of the valley. Even on "good" days, November skies usually contain plenty of clouds, and a ledge high on the hill is the perfect spot from which to watch the clouds change colors every few moments as they are set afire by the vanishing sun.

When the sun is gone, it is time to head home. That means a climb down in the gathering dusk, but twilight, too, is part of the magic of this season.

Suddenly, there is a sharpness to the air, a chill unnoticed a few minutes earlier. The jacket discarded when the sawing and chopping worked up a sweat feels good again. Before leaving, I pile the wood in neat stacks for later hauling. I'm always a little surprised that not more wood was cut, and I say I'll have to avoid some of the distractions tomorrow. But I know I won't.

59

Legacies in Stone

CELLAR HOLES. CHIMNEYS. Stone-lined wells. Dams. Millraces. Maybe a rusting iron kettle. Or some ancient glass bottle.

This is the time I go looking. When the leaves come down, drawing away the curtain of the forest, I can explore. I can visit some of the abandoned home sites that are sprinkled about our woods. I can briefly touch base with those who tried to farm this rocky soil a hundred, two hundred years ago.

It can be intriguing. And bewildering.

The sites are not hard to find. They are all over New England woods. Sometimes you can locate a cellar hole by examining a network of stone walls and figuring out where a house would have been. Sometimes all you have to do is follow one of the old brush-choked roads that wander through the forest. Sometimes you just stumble upon them.

At first, when I was a newcomer to New England, it was the stone walls that fascinated me. So many. So long. So much work. I still find them impressive, but over the years I have found myself looking beyond the walls more and more.

Next it was the cellar holes. Examining the cellars became a favorite fall and winter pastime. Some of the cellars, of course, are not much more than tumbled and jumbled masses of rocks. There are others, however, that are truly works of art. Large trees are often growing out of them now —so many years have passed since their abandonment—but the walls remain straight and solid. In many cellars, there are shelves and cubby-holes built into the walls with flat stones. Care is evident. Craftsmanship is superb.

I particularly like the cellars with large fireplace foundations in the center. In a few cases, the fireplaces are still intact; in fewer cases, the entire chimney remains.

The builders may have left the land a hundred years ago. The wooden walls vanished a decade or two later. Trees sprouted where people once lived. But the stone remains, a monument to the skill of the forgotten farmers.

Bottle collectors searched most of these cellar holes long before I came along. But occasionally I still find an unbroken relic. Maybe a bottle of some patent medicine; maybe horse liniment.

Last winter, I ran across a huge cast-iron kettle just a few yards from a cellar hole I had never visited before. It must have held 25 gallons or more. Immediately, I began trying to figure out its use. Was it for making soap? Making lard? Boiling maple sap? Washing clothes? Cooking? Maybe all of them; maybe none. The kettle is cracked and rusting, but it is still there. Another relic.

Several years ago I found a chimney standing alone in a woods, and that one has baffled me more than the iron kettle. There was no cellar, no stone walls, no well, not even a road nearby. The chimney, with a small fireplace below, was on a knoll in a grove of youngish oaks. Apparently the cabin that had housed it was quite small and, since there was no well, probably was not a permanent home. Maybe it was a hunting cabin. Maybe it had once been surrounded by maples and was a sugar-house. Maybe it was just somebody's hideaway. I don't think I'll ever know, but it's fun to speculate.

I know of another chimney, standing high on a hill. This one is larger and of much more recent vintage. Considerable cement was used in its construction, which automatically decreases its charm in my eyes, but its location is wonderful. The house must have commanded a panoramic view of the area. Even now, once the leaves of the surging forest are gone, I can see for miles from that spot, over villages and valleys, streams and farms. It must have been inspiring to live up there, but I cannot imagine what the owners did for a living. That hill is virtually all boulders; farming it, even by 18th century New England standards, would have been close to impossible.

Lately I've become more and more intrigued by the wells I find near cellar holes. Most are hidden these days beneath large, flat stones, but they are worth a bit of a search. They, too, are works of art. All are round shafts about three feet across, and each is lined from bottom to top with flat stones. They represent, to me, both the value of water and the industriousness of the old homesteaders. Simply digging in that rocky land had to be backbreaking, but to dig deep enough, by pick and shovel, for an ample supply of water, and then to construct the hundreds of rows of stone, around and around . . . well, people just don't work that hard anymore.

Builders of the numerous gristmills and sawmills along the streams and ponds have my respect for the same reasons. There, so many large stones were cut and then pushed and heaved into place. Long sluices were cut through the bottom lands, where rocks and boulders must have blocked every foot. Just building the millraces must have taken weeks, maybe months. But those men persevered, and even though the millers are as forgotten now as the farmers, their legacy remains. It is a silent legacy, but at the same time most eloquent.

60

A Reminder and a Promise

Now I START seeing them, those long, pouch-like nests of orioles. They are a reminder. They are a promise.

The birds themselves—the brightly colored, sweet-singing oriole— don't really spend much time here. They arrive when spring is in full bloom, usually in late April, and then pull out relatively early. They have been gone for a couple of months already.

But it isn't until November, when the leaves are stripped away from the tall trees, that their nests are revealed. And those nests can be as valuable in their own way as the birds' orange feathers and sunrise sere-nades. The nests remind us of a summer that was and a spring that will be again. And in November and December, as we head into what sometimes seems an endless winter, those assurances are indeed needed. We will have new flowers blooming again. We won't have to listen only to the jeering crows and quarrelsome jays forever. Orioles and springtime will come once more.

Each autumn, when most of the leaves are down, I take a casual oriole census of my area. And each year, it seems, I'm pleasantly surprised by how many nests I find. Sure, I heard the orioles singing in May and June, and saw them occasionally flashing as if on fire in the sunlight, but not that many. It's good to know they were here, even if I didn't always notice them at the time.

The other day, on a stroll of perhaps a mile, I found six nests. One was suspended in a small maple, above the edge of a little pond. Two others—not more than 100 feet apart—were in similar maples along a road that curled around another pond. One was high in a tree close to a stream, and the fifth was even higher, perhaps 70 or 80 feet above the ground, dangling from a huge old maple beside a path I walk nearly every day.

As a matter of fact, most of the nests were along routes I walked dozens of times without suspecting orioles might be living there. It's always amazing that birds so colorful, birds that sing so powerfully, can be so secretive.

The sixth nest was the best discovery of all. It was high in an oak tree on a ridge, where we often saw orioles before the area between it and the river was bulldozed during a sand-and-gravel operation. In any other year, I would have expected a nest there. This time, I was happily surprised. It shows that the orioles were not turned off by the bare ground below. It's encouraging that orioles came back after all the earth-shaking noises and ruthless scraping and the loss of bushes and trees.

No other bird in our part of the country can compete with the female oriole in nest-making. She patiently weaves a pouch, perhaps eight or nine inches long, with grasses and plant fibers and always hangs it from one of the top branches of her chosen tree. Often, it takes her a week or more to finish the task. The male can't help—he's too busy singing.

The male, of course, is what we think of when orioles are mentioned. Not only does he greet the spring and summer mornings with his loud, rippling song, but he possesses those orange and black and white feathers that are just as spectacular as his tunes. The female is far less conspicuous. She's more a faded yellow than orange, and doesn't spend her time serenading the world. She's the engineer. She has a nest to build.

Now, long after the eggs have been hatched, the broods raised to adults and the entire family gone back south, the oriole nests are revealed. Each year, when I begin finding them, I think how interesting it would be to watch one being built, and maybe keep an eye on the comings and goings as the parents work to keep the hungry youngsters fed. But I seldom notice the nests in summer.

That's by design, of course. If I could see those nests from down here on the ground, other birds and animals could find them too and the eggs and youngsters would be in great jeopardy. No, it's better this way. Let them raise their families in peace. I'll wait until November to check the nests.

I'll look up at them occasionally as winter progresses. Eventually, they'll get tattered in the wind and rain and snow, and maybe shred away to nothing. But by that time, winter itself may be tattered, too, and the orioles could be heading this way again. I'll be thinking of their return. That's not quite the same as listening to their songs, but almost. It's a promise.

61

Wind and Waves

THE NOISE SURROUNDS ME, dominating the senses. These are sounds—rapid-fire, ever-changing roars and crashes—that I can feel and see almost as distinctly as I hear them. Two of Earth's elemental forces, wind and water, are combining their efforts, and at the same time competing with each other. This is the beach as winter approaches.

I'm sitting on an immense rock, huddled up against an icy, cutting, screaming wind. The waves are slamming ashore, perhaps 15 feet below me. The spray, flashing white in the late-day sunshine, lunges upward onto the ancient rock, like some tentacled creature reaching up from the depths, seeking to pull me into the sea. Before the water can drain back down, the next breaker explodes into the rock. Again and again, on and on.

This is when I'm most mesmerized by the sea. I want the waves wild and alive. I like the might of the ocean. I find the churning, tumultuous sea both stimulating and satisfying. This is my kind of beach day.

I see four small birds flying low over the waves. I have binoculars hanging from my neck, but don't use them; that would mean taking my hands out of my pockets, and it's too cold for that. Instead, I concentrate on a large gray gull that seems to be frolicking in the wind. It flies low, parallel to the shore, for a few hundred feet, and then swoops up into the gale, spreads its wings wide, and lets itself be blown upward and seaward for several moments. Then it dives low and begins the whole routine again.

When the cold starts seeping through my coat and stiffening my joints, I climb off the rock and head back up the beach. The sand is smooth and

firm, and nearly deserted. Far ahead, a woman appears, but in a few minutes she turns and hurries back to the warmth of her car. I'm glad she gave up; I prefer to complete this visit without human interruption.

Gulls, scores of them, are gathered at the edge of the water in a sheltered cove. Most are hunched virtually motionless, standing parallel to the shore, facing the wind. Some fly a few feet into the air as I approach and then quickly drop back to the sand. Others simply wade a few steps into the shallow water as I pass. There are a few half-hearted cries of protest at my intrusion, but nothing like the raucous din such a flock would create in summer. The wind has stolen their bravado.

Farther up the beach, away from the other birds, I see five sandpiper-like birds working the tide line. They're dunlins, light-colored birds that follow the surf in and out, almost as if attached to the water by a string. As the waves crash ashore, they retreat up the sand, carefully staying a few inches ahead of the hissing spray; then, as the water recedes, they dart back with it, repeatedly pecking at minute organisms only they can see. I watch, fascinated that while they never seem to look at the waves, they never get doused. I've had to leap at the last second several times to avoid wet feet.

Sand is blowing across the beach, reminding me of light snow drifting over a pasture. The sand forms miniature drifts behind every obstacle—

pebbles, bits of driftwood, even a feather—just as snow mounds form on the lee side of fence posts and saplings and boulders.

I should turn and go up to the car, but I'm reluctant to leave. I stand, braced against the wind and the invisible bullets of sand it is shooting at me, and marvel once more at all the sounds of the sea. There are the roars and rolling, thunderous booms, yes—but also whispers and splashes and some gurgles that seem almost placid. No two breakers are alike.

Right now, I can understand those who must live near the sea. Much of my life has been spent a thousand miles from it, and I'm still more at home in the woods and fields. But on days like this, when the sea is seething with life and raw, primitive might, I find it entrancing. Today, this is where I must be.

62

Rusty

It WILL BE a different winter. I doubt if my walks in the snow will be as enjoyable as in other years. Rusty is gone.

For the last ten years or so, he has been my companion on nearly every walk. This golden retriever, who was more red than golden, had two chief purposes in life: to protect our yard—which he considered his yard—and to roam the woods with me. I'm wondering how I'll continue walking without him, or if I'll want to.

I've been reluctant to write of his death—putting it in print makes it so coldly "official." But he's been mentioned here too often for his passing to be ignored. And, in reality, he's been too much a part of me and my activities.

We don't know exactly how old he was at the end. He was already an adult when we got him, and although we were told he was two years old at the time, I've always suspected he was older. But whether he was 12 or 15 or whatever, his time went too quickly. It just doesn't seem right that something that enjoyed life so much should have so little of it allotted to him.

We knew his time was coming, of course. He had aged rapidly in the last two years. Overnight, it seemed, he went from a robust dog in his prime to a grizzled patriarch snoozing in the sunshine. Arthritis crept into his hind legs. His hearing slipped. His eyesight started failing.

But his enthusiasm for the woods never diminished. Right to the end, whenever he saw I had on my hiking boots, he begged to go along. It would take him a while, now, to get to his feet, but his tail would be thumping and his eyes would temporarily lose the dullness of age. The flesh may have been weak, but the spirit was more than willing. Finally, though, it became so painful watching him try to get his stiff, aching joints to work that I would sometimes sneak away from the house—just so he wouldn't make the effort.

On one of our last walks together, as we were coming down from the rocky hill we must have climbed 500 times over the years, I noticed Rusty was trotting along passively behind me. That was a first; before, he always had to be out front. It hadn't been a long walk—a concession to his age, and possibly mine—but weariness radiated from every part of his being.

Except his eyes. When I stopped to pat his head, his eyes shone with contentment. It was as if he knew the end was near, and he was glad we had gone up the hill one last time.

Rusty was the perfect companion for somebody like me. Not only was he always ready to go—at midnight, in a snowstorm, in 90 degrees— but it made no difference to him where we went. Oh, he did have opinions, and had a way of showing them. When he came to a fork in a trail, he would go a few yards up the branch he preferred, and wait there until I reached the junction and made my decision. If I chose his route, he'd smugly trot ahead. If I picked the other branch, he'd hurry to overtake me, and then resume his exploration as happily as before.

I'm a slow walker and frequently stop when I find something of interest. Rusty didn't mind my plodding pace—he'd often come back to check on me—but he never understood stopping: a walk was for walking. If I was standing still, looking over some plant or inspecting a bird's nest, he'd cock his head and give me the most quizzical look. I could almost hear him thinking, "*Now* what is he doing?"

If I sat down, he was even more bewildered. First, he'd come back and walk all the way around me, trying to figure out what was holding me there. Then he'd lie down and watch for a few moments. If I remained sitting, he'd then poke his nose under my arm, urging me to get going. If that didn't work, he'd whimper softly. If I still didn't rise, he'd give up for a while, stretch out on the ground, rest his head on his front paws, and wait. But his eyes never seemed to leave my face.

As I look back now, all the trips and miles seem to blur. But the seasons had their distinctions for Rusty. He loved plunging into snow-banks, but needed help when the snow packed into painful ice pellets between his foot pads. Summer walks were tough for him, because of his long hair, and he'd cool off in every body of water we'd come across, whether it was a river—in which he'd submerge everything but his head and tail—or a mud puddle—in which he'd have to lie down to get more than his toes wet.

We often retraced the same trails, but he treated each walk like some exciting new adventure. Nor did his optimism ever wane: he expected to find a rabbit in every clump of weeds, a fox in every rock pile, a woodchuck in every hole in the ground. We might not see an animal of any kind for a dozen walks in a row, but so what? The next trip would be great. I often wish people had his outlook on life.

Rusty had his faults around the house. For one thing, he was a little overzealous in protecting us—so much so that friends referred to him as "that beast." Also, he usually chose the living-room carpet to lie on when pulling the burrs from his tail. And he never understood what was wrong with coming into the house with muddy paws, or why he was banished after rolling in some, uh, ripened carcass that he had found.

But on the trail, he was the most compatible, the most agreeable partner I've ever had. He willingly mirrored my moods. If I wanted to slide on ice like a kid, he would dash along, barking like a puppy. If I spent an entire walk mentally mired in some problem, he'd keep his distance, as if not wanting to disturb my concentration.

All along, I knew time was closing in on us. I recall an afternoon shortly after one of my birthdays when we walked somewhere through the snow. I was thinking of ages and years, and with a little multiplication realized that Rusty and I were entering our middle ages at the same time. It was almost comforting at the moment.

But now he's gone, far too soon. And I find I'm not prepared for his death, after all. I feel he has been cheated somehow—that he should be out there romping through the leaves and snow one more time.

It will feel strange roaming around without my old friend. But maybe, in a way, he'll always be there.

63

Giving Thanks

THINK ABOUT THIS for a moment: if you were to institute your own Thanksgiving Day, when would it be? Somehow, I don't think many of us would do as the Pilgrims did in giving their thanks in late autumn.

Wouldn't most of us, if we were to invent Thanksgiving Day now, put it in spring, when we could celebrate the end of another winter? Or maybe we would choose early summer, when we have all those weeks of sunshine and beach visits and golf games stretching out ahead of us. Late November, often bleak and blustery, heralds only bleaker and more blustery months. It would not rank very high among special times of the year with most of us, would it?

But those early Americans with the big hats and dark dresses and buckles on their shoes saw things a little differently. They lived closer to the soil beneath their feet, and probably closer to a supreme being above them as well.

Thanksgiving was first celebrated in New England because this tough little band of immigrants had had what they considered a pretty good year in a hostile wilderness. The toil of spring and summer had paid off in a harvest that they figured could carry them through winter. For that they were extremely grateful.

I suppose the idea of when to give thanks depends on priorities, on what is important in our lives. The Pilgrims were struggling for the essentials: a roof and walls, food and warmth. They had to chop out trees and brush to make fields, and then found the soil stony and stubborn. They had to stalk wild beasts for food. They knew what a New England winter held in store. Their provisions, grown and gathered so carefully, would dwindle far too quickly. Snow and ice would be constant enemies. Wind would howl through their huts, cold would seep into their very bones. There would be sickness. There would be death.

In that environment, priorities become clear in a hurry. All the Pilgrims could think of, and work for, and pray for, was survival. What else mattered?

I've occasionally wondered if, indeed, they did hold another day of thanksgiving—when spring finally came. Maybe there was too much work to do then to set aside a day for celebration, but men and women of their beliefs must have thought deeply, while wrestling with stumps or spinning wool, how blessed they were to be still alive and able to pursue their dreams for a future.

Anyway, as I made one of my evening strolls along the river recently, I was trying to decide when I would put my own Thanksgiving Day. I tried mentally listing the things I was grateful for, and quickly found that those I would put at the top of the list could be observed at any time of year: warm and enduring friendships, healthy and happy children, and the love, understanding and lifetime companionship of a special woman. No one day of thanks could do justice to their value.

Nor, I decided, could I find a specific time that would best symbolize how important it is to have the mountains and seashore and forests and rivers close at hand, and the time to learn what they have to teach, to enjoy the experiences they offer. I'm thankful, too, that I still get to see

butterflies and hawks, that I can hear foxes yipping in the moonlight and bluebirds singing in ecstasy, that I can smell lilacs in full bloom and hay curing in the June sunshine. Rainbows and thunderstorms are on the list, and so are softly falling snow and sugar maples in riotous colors and waves crashing ashore and a deer at the brook and otters on the ice.

All of these things whirled through my mind as I walked, and then it occurred to me that perhaps what we should be thankful for, as much as anything else, are those early Pilgrims and others of our ancestors, not only for their ability to endure but for the ideals they held to through deadly difficult times. Freedom of thought. Faith in their convictions. Courage to explore, to expand horizons. Strength enough to build a nation based on freedom and faith and courage.

For those things, it doesn't really matter when we observe Thanksgiving Day—just that we have one, and remember why.

64

Fury of the Shrew

SOMEWHERE IN THE computer design of shrews there must have been a glitch. They were programmed well, for the most part, to compete in their frantic, violent world, but there was a breakdown. It's as if the last page of the program were garbled; the ending just isn't right.

Shrews are tough little animals that resemble pointy-headed mice. They're our smallest mammals—rarely weighing more than an ounce—and they spend their entire lives trying only to survive, seeking enough to eat without being killed by larger animals. That's the challenge for most small wild creatures, but there is an ironic twist to the shrews' story.

By being numerous, active and so small, shrews would seem natural prey for every hunter from weasels to owls, from foxes to house cats. And they are. Even snakes and bullfrogs and large bass kill the varieties of shrews that frequent waterways. So to help even the odds a bit, shrews were given a special defense mechanism: a highly repulsive odor.

This is where the glitch took place. The odor is strong enough to keep most of the predators from eating the shrews—but it doesn't stop them from killing the little things. That doesn't seem quite right, does it? Every time I come across a dead shrew in the woods or fields, I think of what a mean trick was played on these animals. What good is a defense mechanism that kicks in only during death throes?

I usually think then, too, of monarch butterflies. As the big orange-and-black butterflies slowly migrate down the East Coast each fall, they should be snapped out of the air by the birds. But they aren't, because somehow the birds know that monarchs taste lousy.

If word got around about how terrible shrews smell, wouldn't they have a better chance of lasting more than a few months? Maybe they need a publicity campaign. Or an adjustment in their, uh, stench-producing process. Skunks might be able to give them a few tips.

In reality, of course, I know this all works out for the best. Like mice and mosquitoes and rabbits and a hundred other species, shrews would quickly get out of hand if not for the predators.

Far more shrews are around than most people realize. They're not seen all that often, because they live down there amid the leaves and rocks and roots that are half under and half on top of the soil's surface. And it's usually in the darkness that they venture above ground. During the day, they do their hunting in mole tunnels and mouse runways and other out-of-sight places.

But even when not seen, shrews are in motion. Their entire lives seem to be switched to fast-forward. With heartbeats and breathing rates that both approach 800 per minute—much faster than a hummingbird's—the shrews burn up energy so quickly they have to eat almost constantly.

Late autumn seems to be the time when most dead shrews are found. One reason is that much of their food supply—such as earthworms, insects, spiders, snails, centipedes, young birds and baby mice—is harder to find when cold weather arrives. The scarcity forces the shrews to venture more often into the open and leaves them far more vulnerable to attack.

Not all the deaths are caused by teeth and talons. Shrews are so high-strung, so tightly wound, that they often go into shock when attacked or chased—they can be literally scared to death. That, I suppose, might be considered a justified end for something that does so much terrorizing of its own down there on the forest floor.

Still, I can't help feeling there is something out of kilter here. Nature doesn't waste things; it just doesn't work that way.

But maybe the shrews do serve a purpose. Maybe there are times when a little shrew left on a hillside or in a barren field is later gobbled up. It might be all that saves other hunters from starving. I would imagine that if an animal is hungry enough, it wouldn't care about odor. Is that what it's all about? I wonder.

65

Snow Fascination

It's still there. I know this is strange, and it probably marks me as some sort of eccentric, but my fascination with new snow hasn't diminished yet. Each winter I expect it to dissipate, or at least lessen, but it's still there.

Don't get me wrong; I get as weary of snow and winter as everybody else. To my way of thinking, winter is supposed to end in February, but it never does. March should be spring, but it never is. And I don't like slushy snow or dirty snow at all.

But give me a fresh cover of spotless snow, and the old exhilaration bubbles up again. When I awake to such a snowfall, I resent having to go to work, not because of slippery roads and parking problems, but because I want to be out there in the snow. Just like a kid. Apparently, I haven't grown up yet. I wonder if I ever will.

This infatuation with new snow goes back as far as I can remember. My father used to have to pry me out of bed on cold winter mornings, until he discovered a magic phrase: "It snowed during the night." That would wake me up instantly, and I'd hurry to get outside before Dad.

I wanted to be the first person to walk in that snow, the first to leave tracks. There was an excitement to being the first, something akin to exploring new lands, going where no person has gone. If anybody beat me to it, some of the magic was lost.

We had a dog in those days that shared my enthusiasm for the snow. The heavier the snow, the more he loved it, and he'd roll in the snow and leap about in sheer ecstasy. Both of us enjoyed plunging into a drift that always appeared between the house and barn. I'd flounder around there with the dog until Dad came out and suggested we get to the milking.

When I became interested in wildlife, fresh snow was my means of learning what was around the farm. Pheasants and foxes and mice in the fields. Rabbits and squirrels and weasels in the woods. Muskrats and raccoons along the stream. I didn't see the animals often, but their stories —where they went and what they did—were written there in the snow. All I had to do was go looking.

Other benefits of new snow became evident, too, as time went on. I liked the way the snow hid the scars of the countryside, the bulldozed woodlots and desolate sandbanks and ugly roadside litter. Snow never cured these ills, of course, but for a few hours the wounds would seem bandaged, the land temporarily clean and new.

Mostly, though, it was the old illusion of being first that made me a snow walker, and I suppose that's still the strongest attraction. When there are no other human footprints, when there are no tire tracks on the lanes, every forest and field becomes a pristine wilderness. Nobody has been there; it's all mine to explore.

All these years, I've kept expecting my enthusiasm to wane. Other people my age are planning moves to Florida. Many openly despise winter. Snow is nothing but a nuisance, they tell me—an expensive and dangerous headache. And there are times, I agree, when snow turns to dirty, dingy slush.

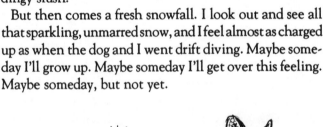

But then comes a fresh snowfall. I look out and see all that sparkling, unmarred snow, and I feel almost as charged up as when the dog and I went drift diving. Maybe someday I'll grow up. Maybe someday I'll get over this feeling. Maybe someday, but not yet.

66

December Sunsets

First, THE HEAVY CLOUD flashed a brilliant red-orange, as if ignited, for just a minute or two. Then it glowed, turning a softer, fuchsia shade that reminded me of embers just after the flames are gone. Again, the moment was fleeting. Gold, purple and pink quickly streaked across the sky.

We—a young son and I—stood there watching. We had been cutting firewood on the hillside and had just gathered up the tools for the long walk back to the house. It had been a productive, satisfying afternoon, but now light was fading in the woods. It would be dark by the time we climbed down from the steep, rocky slope and followed the river path home.

Then the color show began in the west, and the boy and I walked to a bulging outcropping and watched. Neither of us said a word; we both simply felt the same pull at the same time. We had to linger and watch this sunset. We just had to.

That day was several years ago. I wonder if my son, who is no longer a boy, remembers. It was about this time of year, when twilight and sunset seem to take on special qualities. Not every sunset, of course, is that spectacular—if it happened often, it wouldn't be special—but for some reason there are a few more of them as autumn slides toward winter.

It takes clouds as well as sunshine for the most elaborate sunsets, and perhaps that's why they occur more often now. On many days in late fall, the clouds hang heavy, as if already carrying burdens of snow. They're ominous, almost angry—until that magical moment of sunset. Then they, become things of incredible beauty.

When that moment arrives, usually just as the sun is slipping below the horizon, clouds lying low in the west catch fire. Dark clouds turn purple, often fringed with gold. Sometimes, they turn redder by the second until the entire heavens are glowing. Next, there may be dozens of shades of crimson, orange and pink before they burn down to embers. I don't think the metaphor of fire is farfetched; the best sunsets really do suggest wildfire in the sky.

Clouds appear to move faster now, scudding across the sky, usually whirling away from the setting sun. They are being bullied by the wind, and each twist, each movement of the clouds contributes to the ever-changing colors. On certain days, a cloud can run through nearly every color of the rainbow in ten minutes.

I still occasionally climb around on that slope my son and I went to. Sometimes I go up there to check on a fox that has a den under the outcropping. Sometimes I go looking for partridges, or to pick up hickory nuts. And once or twice, in November or December, I go up there just to see the sunset.

It's the best place I know of in my area for watching the color shows. Not only does the high ridge face west, but it looks across a quiet river toward a treed horizon beyond. The water provides reflections of molten gold or liquid rose. The trees across the way add the dark silhouettes that make the sky look even brighter than it is.

In a way, the outcropping has become a little retreat for me. It's a place of silence, a place of contemplation. At this time of year, it can also be windy and cold, but I can take the discomfort for a little while if the payoff is fire in the sky. I'm not sure any of the shows have matched the first one I shared with my son—that one was awesome and eerie, almost unreal—but some have come close.

And when there is a particularly stunning sunset, I climb down thinking about the day a man and a small boy stood up there mesmerized. I hope he remembers it, too.

67

Ice Needles

Go out at just the right time these days, to the right places, under the right conditions, and you can find the ice needles. They are something to see.

There's a good chance you'll get chilled, of course, but anybody who appreciates natural phenomena should see the needles at least once.

The right time usually is late afternoon, about the time sunshine vanishes and the temperature starts dropping.

The right places are the small, shallow pools—puddles, really—where there is just a tiny amount of open water surrounded by rocks, weeds and saplings.

The right conditions include, first and foremost, an absolute stillness to the air. No hint of breeze. A clear sky helps, too; clear dusks seem to drop the temperature more quickly.

What are ice needles? Well, they are long, straight slivers of ice that reach out from the edge of the pool as the water surface is cooled. They extend from each weed stalk and pebble. They do, indeed, resemble knitting needles and, in effect, they knit the sheet of ice that will cover the pool by morning.

Now, before you say that watching ice form must be as exciting as watching grass grow, hold on a minute. The needles, and the patterns they create, are simply beautiful. Like snowflakes, they seem never to fashion the same design twice and are just as delicate.

Starting slowly, as tiny fingers, the slivers stretch out at various angles—I doubt if scientists can explain why each goes its own way—and as they lengthen, they crisscross numerous times, leaving intricate patterns even after the spaces between the needles are filled in with the oh-so-thin ice.

In early stages, when they may be a foot long but no wider than a knitting needle, the ice slivers are so fragile that any breeze that might ripple the water even minutely would destroy them. In fact, I feel that even words spoken out loud would shatter the needles.

After perfect ice nights, meaning that the stillness remained all night and the temperature dropped to only about 25 degrees, I sometimes return to the little pools. Another fantastic sight often awaits.

The pool's iced surface will be glass smooth, so the lines and angles of the needles can be seen through the ice. After admiring the patterns from above, break a section of ice free and turn it upside down. Sometimes those lines extend down an inch or two, forming exquisite paper-thin triangles and rectangles, and even pentagons and hexagons, depending on how the needles lie. Each is incredibly fragile, incredibly beautiful.

Just how they are formed is no easier for me to comprehend than how snowflakes become so intricate, but it's mostly a matter of congelation and condensation. The formations are always best in pools so shallow that a cover of ice takes virtually all the water. In such puddles, the otherwise hollow space between the ice and the ground can hold some intriguing sights.

Ice has other moments of beauty, too. It may not be lovely when it makes highways treacherous, or when it snaps power lines, but even the most blase can admire the flowery patterns it paints on windows on certain mornings.

Hoarfrost is another example. There are a few dawns each winter when every branch and limb and weed is sheathed in sparkling crystallized ice. It happens most often along open streams, and it usually takes a severe plunge in temperature, along with ideal atmospheric conditions, for the formations to be at their best. Like the ice needles, hoarfrost is exceedingly delicate and vanishes in moments when hit by sunshine.

And there are the ice flowers. Also hoarfrost, they "grow" on frozen ponds from vapors or mists that drift across clear ice from some patch of open water. They are infinitely varied, sometimes several inches high, sometimes minute. They may resemble miniature ferns or an arrangement of the softest feathers. The only things they all have in common are their color—a pure, dazzling white—and their spectacular beauty.

Unfortunately, finding the fragile flowers is pretty much a matter of luck and persistence. You may walk frozen ponds each morning of the winter and never find one. But that fact only makes them even more worthy of the search.

Ice flowers are something to look for later in the winter. Right now, ice needles are a little easier to find, and they are enough. If we have to have winter, they are not a bad way at all for it to start.

68

The Sycamore

MOST TREES LOOK miserable in winter, don't they? Stripped of their leaves, standing dark and forlorn, they seem to shiver in the cold wind. But not the sycamores; they are probably more attractive now than at any other time of year.

Sycamores certainly stand out more now than in other seasons. The unique mottled, splotchy patterns of their bark are revealed when the leaves are dropped. There is no other bark quite like it. The sycamores' basic whiteness fairly gleams in the December sunshine, particularly when seen against a background of a gray hillside or stark, empty fields.

Still, it is more than the color of the sycamores that makes them special. Some of the birches are white, too, and though stirring in their own way, the birches never quite measure up to the sycamores. Not to me; not here.

The truly magnificent paper birches grow in the north country, in the mountains. The largest birches in southern New England are not even wild; they were planted in yards, as ornamentals, and that puts them into a different category.

Sycamores sometimes were planted, too, of course—they're great shade trees—but the trees I find really alluring are the old giants standing along streams and rivers. Once in a while, there will be a sycamore in a field, or perhaps on a hillside, but most of them are in the bottom lands, standing guard over the icy waterways, just as they have done for decades. They seem so much more at home out there, in the wild; they look out of place when surrounded by concrete and buildings and fences.

When I think of sycamores, I think of wild animals. Sycamores have

a tendency to decay from within, and that leaves a great many hollow limbs and hollow trunks even while the trees are otherwise thriving. Animals love hollow trees; the trees provide dens and nesting sites and places of shelter. Squirrels, raccoons, opossums, skunks, bats, owls and probably many other creatures use the cavities in old sycamores to sleep away the winter or simply wait out storms. One large tree can serve several animals of several varieties.

The sycamores are special for another reason, too. Throughout the winter, they display their seed capsules for next year in the round clusters sometimes called buttonballs dangling from the tips of branches. It can be encouraging, especially when the snow piles up and the wind howls, to see those seed clusters. They mean that spring will come again. There are times every winter when we need such assurances.

Yet I'm wondering how long we will have the sycamores. There was a time when they were the largest trees in New England, taller than the elms, broader than the largest oaks, with crowns more far-reaching than the chestnuts'. In fact, some of the sycamores were so large they almost defy comprehension: up to 20 feet in diameter, 125 feet tall, with tops of 150 feet across. They were so immense that early explorers often used hollow sycamores as temporary shelters, and there are numerous records of homesteaders using the largest trunks as buildings, sometimes as houses. Fantastic trees.

There are no sycamores of that size these days. The largest one I've seen in southern New England stands beside a river in Connecticut. It has a circumference of more than 23 feet; the diameter is probably seven or eight feet. I've never seen one in Rhode Island more than six feet through its trunk.

It's possible that the sycamores could someday go the way of our other mighty trees of the past. Elms that once towered over riverbanks and shaded a great many village streets have been gone for years; it's hard to find even a skeleton still standing these days. Diseases destroyed them, just as blight nearly wiped out the native chestnuts. There are still some chestnuts around now, but most are mere saplings compared with the giants of yesterday, and few of these young trees will survive long enough to reach half the size of their ancestors before the blight hits them, too.

Diseases have hurt the sycamores, too, and so have the side effects of civilization. The rich soil that sycamores favor also made the best farmland, so the massive trees were removed. Clearing land and thinning wood lots also left the remaining sycamores vulnerable to wind and ice storms and floods. And I'm sure the acid rain of the present will play a negative role in the trees' future.

For now, though, we still have the sycamores. They may be a bit smaller than those of a few hundred years ago, but they still have that curious, multicolored bark that stands out like a beacon in the winter woods. They still have the stretching branches and the sheltering holes for raccoons and squirrels. Through the worst of winter they still promise the return of spring. Sycamores still are special.

69

Furry Torpedoes

The otters looked like submarines, or maybe torpedoes. They dived into the water, then moments later exploded through the thin ice, blasting upward with a force that threw bits of ice ten feet into the air. They seemed to be taking turns. Again and again. It was quite a show.

Otters are known for their playfulness, but until watching them frolic on a small pond last winter, I had never seen it. In the past few years, I had seen some otters swimming, and once surprised a family of them traveling up a tiny rocky brook. And I'd seen the sliding troughs otters make on snow-covered slopes.

But until last winter, I had always missed the fun itself. And I thought I was going to miss it again—it seemed everybody in town had seen the

otters except me. I heard about them for several weeks, in the hardware store, at the bank, at basketball games. A photographer friend even showed me pictures he'd taken. I started driving out to the otters' pond almost every evening; I found plenty of tracks, and twice saw leftover fragments of fish on the ice, but no otters.

Not many years ago, merely finding otter tracks would have been something. Once among the big targets of trappers, otters had been all but wiped out here. And trapping was only one of the reasons for the decline; water pollution, wetland filling and forest destruction played major roles, too.

But the otters have been back for some time now. There are far more of them around than most people realize; even as active as they are, they can live nearby without giving away their presence. Only in winter do otters really show themselves.

They apparently cannot resist tobogganing and ice-sliding. Just like kids. And, just like kids, they seem willing to go to any lengths for their fun. On a snowy morning last winter, I followed an otter's tracks from one small pond to another. The animal could have made the journey quickly and easily; instead, it detoured to a high, wooded ridge—nearly tripling its trip—then slid 40 feet down the slope to the water. Perhaps the toboggan ride wasn't the only reason for the detour, but it would be hard to convince me of that.

On other walks last winter, I came across tracks that showed how otters, when traveling over snow-covered ice, frequently run a few steps and then dive headlong, sliding as far as possible. I even found the trail of one otter that went almost half a mile along a stream by zigzagging up and down the shoreline slope, climbing four or five feet at a time and then sliding back down. The otter must have had a ball.

But I didn't get to see it.

I knew my best chance would be at the pond near town, and eventually perseverance paid off. Bettie and I swung by there on a Saturday morning and, finally, spotted an otter lying on the ice, contentedly munching on a fish.

We stopped. In moments the real show began. Another otter pulled a larger fish out of the water, and the otters began tussling. But it looked more like a friendly wrestling match than a fight. Eventually, both dived into the water and left the fish on the ice.

About then, the ice breaking began. One after another, where the ice was thin, four otters appeared. Each one crashed through the ice from below, each one sending ice particles flying in all directions. Sometimes they waited until all four were on the surface before they submerged and went at it again.

Then some person slammed a car door—we hadn't noticed that three other cars had also stopped—and the otters vanished.

I've been looking forward to the return of snow and ice ever since.

70

How Do They Know?

It's a question I seem to be asking myself often when thinking about wildlife. There always seem to be little incidents popping up that defy explanation. Now, as the wind howls outside, it might be a good time to sit by the fire and ponder these things.

How, for instance, do the goldfinches know when we put out thistle seed? There hadn't been a goldfinch around the yard for months before we hung a bag of their favorite seeds from the clothes line. Within hours, a whole flock of them arrived and immediately began working the bag, three or four at a time. Where did they come from? Who told them we had thistle seed?

What birds would be coming to the feeders if this were 1787 or 1687? Starlings and house sparrows and house finches weren't around here then; they're all introduced species. Cardinals and titmice didn't live in New England then, either; they've moved up from the South relatively recently. Of course, people didn't feed birds much 200 and 300 years ago, and it's possible there would be more native birds around now if we had not started giving handouts to some of these newcomers. I wonder.

I also wonder how the mockingbird, another Southern bird, fares so well up here in the cold and snow. Those around my yard won't even come to the feeders. Even in midwinter, the mockers seem perfectly content with their lives in the bushes and woods' edges. Occasionally, I see them perched right out in the wind, whistling as cheerily as if it were April. Have they grown an extra layer of feathers since they moved North?

How do the gray squirrels know where we store walnuts? Last fall we gathered half a bushel of walnuts and put them in the garage. Weeks

later, the garage door was left open for a day, and the squirrels came in and carried off dozens of nuts. And it wasn't just one squirrel; when we discovered the thieves, there were three in the basket. How did they know? I don't think squirrels had ever been inside the garage before.

And speaking of squirrels, how do the little red squirrels make their snow tunnels so straight? When snow is deep and soft, the pineys sometimes tunnel through it from the cedars to the maple where our feeders hang. It's an uphill distance of 25 or 30 feet, but the tunnels are as straight as if laid out by an engineer with a transit. How do they do that?

How do the grouse know where to find the partridgeberries? The red berries grow on tiny, ground-hugging vines that are easily buried by snow. Yet the grouse or partridges, which seldom bother with the berries until there is snow, seem to have no trouble finding them when hunger time arrives. They scratch away the snow and help themselves. How do they know where to look? Do they remember from one winter to the next?

How do the mallards know when to leave? There are always a few ducks that linger on the ponds and streams far into the winter, even after ice begins forming along the shores. They stay even as their area of open water grows smaller and smaller, yet they vanish on the night when the ice closes in completely. They never get caught by the ice, even when the freeze-up appears sudden. How do they know how cold the night will be?

How do foxes know when the ice is safe? Foxes love to wander over frozen ponds—ice enables them to explore cattail stands and similar places off-limits to them the rest of the year—but has anyone ever seen a fox plunge through thin ice? It happens to dogs; are foxes smarter?

Do the chickadees, which travel through the winter woods in company of a few nuthatches and brown creepers, really rely on the other birds to find food? It appears that way. Chickadees seem to spend all their time socializing while the others, particularly the creepers, are all business, quietly examining the bark of trees for hidden insects. Also, why do the nuthatches probe the tree trunks upside down? Do they ever fall on their heads?

Why are there always a few robins and other supposedly migratory songbirds hiding out in the thickets in winter? What keeps them from defying instinct? Are they rebels or adventurers who want to try something different? Or are they simply too lazy to make the long flights? I know they certainly look miserable during January snowstorms.

Maybe it's only justice that wintering robins have a difficult time. They don't belong here now; they weren't made for New England winters. Of course, that's easy for me to say while stretched out in front of a crackling fire, with stout walls between me and the cold. Would I fare any better than the robins, or as well, if I had to live in the woods right now? That's a question I don't plan to answer.

71

One Tough Bird

It's a bitterly cold morning, the kind that makes that first step outside the house a test of willpower. The wind is howling through the trees; I just know it's going to hit with a raw, icy blast the moment I step outside.

But on days like this, the birds need food to combat the cold, so I bundle up and trudge out to the feeder. Already, the house finches are waiting in the low bushes, hunched up like little old men in overcoats. I see a female cardinal in the spruce, but she seems reluctant to leave the sheltering boughs. As I pour the sunflower seeds into the wooden box, two chickadees come flying from the cedars at the edge of the woods, but even they, usually so exuberant, are silent today. The wind seems to have beaten everything in the yard into submission.

As I turn to hurry back to the house, a clear, cheery whistle comes ringing across the frozen lawn. I know what made that call: a mockingbird. But I still pause to take a look. There he is, perched high in a wild rose bramble just beyond the yard, fully exposed to the wind, apparently as contented as if this were some June morning. What's everybody so gloomy about? Isn't this a refreshing breeze? What an invigorating way to start the day!

In spite of my discomfort, I have to smile just a bit. That mockingbird is one tough character.

There are times when I find the mockers exasperating. Like all those spring and summer mornings when they begin their boisterous singing outside the window long before dawn. And the times when they fool me into thinking there is a new bird in the neighborhood by mimicking the songs of other birds. And when they get a little overly protective of their

nesting territories and chase other birds away.

But in winter, I like mockingbirds. I like their upbeat personalities. I like their resilience. I like their independence. They're never surly, like the starlings and sparrows, birds that endure winter, rather than enjoy it. Mockers are around every day, no matter what the weather. They can be counted on, unlike, say, the colorful evening grosbeaks that invade the yard en masse one day and then disappear for a week. And the mockingbirds are not beggars. I think I like that trait most of all.

At this time of year, virtually all the birds that we see around the yard are there for one reason: to get their share of the handouts. If we did not have a feeder, we would never see evening grosbeaks. Chickadees and house finches and blue jays and titmice and juncos practically live on our sunflower seeds. Goldfinches cannot resist the bag of thistle seeds. Cardinals and doves love the cracked corn we spread on the ground. Downy woodpeckers and nuthatches make dozens of trips each day to the suet, or meat fats, that we hang in the maple.

And the mockingbird? He (or she) snubs it all. The hard little berries on multiflora roses, the cedars, the bittersweet vines along the woods and the sprawling juniper bushes in the meadow are quite enough, thank you. He doesn't need us, and I think he wants us to know that.

A few years ago, after I'd mentioned in an article on feeding birds that mockers did not come to my feeder, several people wrote that they "lured" their mockers with raisins and apples and bits of other fruits. I'm sure that works, but I have no desire even to try luring the mockingbirds anywhere. Why turn such a free-spirited, sassy bird into just another beggar? It's doing just fine on its own.

I've also been told that mockers have a weakness for suet, but so far "my" mockers have never been seen taking suet. Maybe we have too many multiflora roses, which the mockers themselves have planted over the years with seeds in their droppings.

The fact that mockers stand up to our winters so well is in itself one of the more intriguing aspects of these delightful birds. For centuries, there were no mockingbirds in New England. They were limited to the Deep South; in fact, they were something of a symbol of Southern wild-life. Always popular, they were chosen as the state bird of Arkansas, Florida, Mississippi, Tennessee and Texas.

Then, as the climate changed slightly in this century, as our weather warmed up a few degrees, the mockers, along with such birds as cardinals and titmice, extended their ranges northward. One of our region's authorities on birds recalls seeing a mockingbird for the first time in Rhode Island in the mid-1940s. By the mid-'50s, mockingbirds were appearing rather regularly, and by the '60s they were becoming common.

He believes that the increased planting of berry-bearing bushes and trees—along with the milder weather and the rising popularity of back-yard feeders—helped the mockers thrive.

Now, mockingbirds are familiar in most suburban areas, and easy to find in many city yards, as well. Occasionally, the long-tailed gray birds with the distinctive white wing and tail markings can be found at the edges of dense forests; but for the most part they like to stay near humans. Maybe they need an audience for all their songs, whistles and mimicry. Maybe they like being able to grab a few raisins or a bit of suet if the going gets too rough. Maybe it is so that they can jeer at the birds that have to rely on handouts. I don't think the reasons matter. They make our winters so much more lively, I'm just glad they found their way to New England.

72

The Winter Solstice

Today is the winter solstice: the official beginning of winter. That's not good news for those who have little use for snow, ice and cold wind. But there are a couple of ways of beating the depressing thought that we are now descending into months of hostile weather and barren countryside.

First, after today the days will actually begin to lengthen. Not much— it will take a week to add even one minute of daylight. Even though it will get colder before it gets warmer, the increasingly later sunsets should be a small measure of consolation—a bit of assurance that there will be another spring in due time.

The solstice is a milestone, a turning of a corner, but obviously it's not the abrupt beginning of a new season. Only those who would cut the year into four neat little three-month segments see it that way. There is constant overlapping, so much so that even now, as we talk about autumn sliding into winter, we can see signs of spring that were formed last summer.

Which brings us to the second way of beating winter depression. Take a look at the trees and bushes—the dogwoods and rhododendrons and lilacs, in particular: See all the buds just waiting for spring's go-ahead? They seem almost as impatient as we are. The buds won't make the coming weeks any warmer or melt the snow any faster, but like the gradually lengthening days, they are proof that winter won't last forever.

What I find so appealing about the buds is that they both tie everything together—provide the continuity among the seasons—and provide a great deal of hope. All through the sub-zero nights of January and

snowstorms of February, we can look to the buds for comfort.

It's all there already: the promise of another season of greenery, the promise of new life. Today, as winter begins, the buds are assuring us of another spring.

Buds are rather remarkable. They're tightly wrapped packages that carry another cycle of leaf and twig and blossom inside. These packages are formed in summer, well before the leaves drop. On some trees and bushes, the buds are so thick and show so much life by September that I get the feeling it is the new buds that actually cause the leaves to fall — sort of push out the old to make room for the new.

Some buds, like those on the rhododendrons, are already green and fat. They seem very impatient, as if ready to burst open at any moment.

But that won't happen. We're the ones anxious for another spring; plants and trees need winter for resting.

The buds are hibernating now, biding their time, just as the wood-chuck in its den is hibernating. They have their own clock to follow, the one ticking away down in their roots. It will awaken the buds when there is sufficient warmth and light for the sap to start stirring once more, when it is time for the next stage in the cycle.

Lilac buds are among my favorites when I want to look beyond winter. They might even rank ahead of the rhododendrons; though not as large or as "ready" as the rhododendron buds, the lilac buds hint more of rebirth because lilac bushes are otherwise bare. Rhododendrons, by contrast, keep their green leaves all winter, and so never appear in need of rebirth.

Already, on the winter solstice—nearly four months before tiny leaves will appear—the lilacs are sporting healthy buds. In the weeks ahead, those buds may be coated with ice and covered with snow, but they'll still be there, alive and well, when the ice and snow melt. Both persistent and patient, they always outlast winter. It helps just to know that.

Years ago, I planted lilacs around the yard, for their flowers and the heady perfume they exude each May. There was no thought then to the bushes' dormant stage. But now I know the lilacs have another value. They can comfort and inspire—at least a little bit —just when we need it most.

Winter

73

Frozen to a Pump Handle

"As cold as a pump handle in January."

I recently ran across that saying in a book on rural Vermont, and it brought back a lot of memories. Most of them painful. All of them cold.

You see, Vermont isn't the only place where pump handles get cold. Anybody who ever had to stand outside pumping water in the thin, gray light of a Northern winter dawn knows there are no colder jobs on the farm. Milking the cows on those mornings was like a Caribbean vacation compared with filling the water trough.

It was doubly bad for me. Not only did I have to endure the whipping wind and the numbing temperatures, but I usually wound up with my gloves frozen to the pump handle. That can be unbelievably cold. And most humiliating.

For those who've never had that chore, let me explain what filling a water trough on a sub-zero morning involved in the days before electric pumps and automatic heating elements. It's been between 25 and 30 years since I thawed out pumps, but some things you never forget. No matter how hard you try.

On our little farm, in Ohio, there were two troughs for the cows, one inside the barn and the other at the opposite end of the night holding pen, which we called the cowyard. Water for the barn trough had to be carried from a well near the house, a distance of perhaps a hundred yards. The second trough, although farther from the house, had its own well.

Sounds simple, doesn't it?

It wasn't. Not for a ten-year-old boy. Before I could start pumping, I'd have to get the pumps working. And I'd have to break the ice on the troughs. Sometimes, just getting to the barn and cowyard was tougher than anything else. If it had snowed during the night, I could count on high drifts between the house and the barn. Snow in that country always drifted, and the highest drifts on the farm always piled up there. Drifts higher than my head. Mountains of snow. The wind blew the snow across the open fields, swirled it around the corncrib and granary and stacked it up right across my path. I wonder how many unkind words I mumbled about my ancestors for putting those buildings where they did.

I had a choice of breaking a trail through the drifts or going around them. Going through them was more of a challenge, and more fun, but it made carrying buckets of water a bit hazardous. There were plenty of spills, and more than once I spilled the water all over myself, resulting in instant ice on more than just my gloves. But I'm getting ahead of the story.

Dad would get things started before waking me. He'd build a fire in the cookstove and set a bucket of water on it. By the time I had bundled up and pulled on my boots, the water would be hot. The older boys joined Dad in the barn for the milking and feeding—the warm and easy jobs—while I reluctantly faced my responsibilities. Don't get me wrong; I liked farm life. I even liked cows. But nobody could like watering them on January mornings.

Most of the time, I'd trudge out to check the troughs before even trying the pumps, hoping that the cows hadn't been too thirsty during the night, so that the troughs wouldn't need much water. It never worked that way. Unless it had been so cold that the water had frozen early, the tanks were usually about empty. And on those mornings when the ice levels were high, the cows were so thirsty they guzzled up the water as fast as I could pour it. There was no way of winning.

Before adding water, of course, I'd have to break the ice. That could be as easy as rapping it with a baseball bat, or as difficult as slamming it repeatedly with an ax. The first time I used an ax on the trough in the barn, Dad yelled at me to be sure to use the blunt side of the ax head. The trough was of thin metal, and he figured I'd chop a hole right through the bottom. Apparently he didn't have much confidence in my reasoning powers.

Sooner or later, I'd have to get down to the business of thawing out the pumps. The well near the house was usually rather cooperative. Maybe that was because it was in a sheltered spot, or because it was deep, or because it was relatively new. I'm not sure just why, but more often than not I could get it going with one bucket of steaming water, slowly pouring it in the top with one hand while working the long handle up and down with the other.

Of course, sometimes the morning was so cold that the pump would freeze up again before I got back from the barn with the empty buckets.

The other pump was the real problem. Totally exposed to the wind, surrounded by acres of nothingness, it was in the coldest spot on the farm, bar none. In summer, I loved going out there early in the morning, because I could hear the quail whistle from the hayfields and the meadowlarks sing from the fence posts, but in winter I hated that place more than any other I knew. It was my Siberia.

I'd heat water in both buckets before going out there, praying that the old pump would catch before I ran out of hot water. Returning for more water not only prolonged my agony, but also was something of a mark of incompetence, and my brothers always reminded me that they never had to do it. At least that's what they claimed.

So I poured the water most carefully and pumped furiously. Nothing happened with the first bucketful. Except noise. There was a creaking in the handle, and a raucous, hollow sound down in the well. By the time I had started on the second bucket, I'd begin to worry. Already my face was stinging from the cold, my eyes were watering, my toes hurt and my fingers were getting numb. I forced myself to pour more slowly, a mere trickle at a time, but I still spilled enough that it ran down the pump handle. Did you ever try pouring a bucket with one hand? Spilling is easy.

Just when I was sure it would never catch, the pump responded with that deep gurgle that meant success. Immediately, I'd begin feeling the weight of the water, and in seconds the trough would start filling. By the time I'd finished, however, the water that I had spilled down the handle would be ice. I'd be standing there, my gloves frozen to the handle, feeling like an idiot. The only thing worse was having my brothers find out.

74

Fox on the Hill

THE TRACKS STRETCHED away in the fresh snow, a clean, straight line of them. Almost dainty. Along the lane and then across the pond and finally back up the slope. Finding them was far easier than I expected. My fox was still around after all.

As soon as I had noticed it snowing the previous evening, I had known where I would be going first thing in the morning. For several weeks, I had been wondering about the fox—had it pulled out for good?—and now the new snow cover would give me a chance to find out.

Slightly more than a year ago, I wrote of my interest in this phantom-like neighbor, a fox that lived up on a wooded hill near my home. At that time, I had never seen it but had learned a great deal about its habits by following its tracks over the years. I discovered it sometimes followed my tracks, too; it seemed as fascinated by the actions of me and my dog as I was by its lifestyle.

In the last year, I've seen the fox twice, but more recent happenings on the hill had me concerned about its future. More condominiums were coming. That meant another invasion of bulldozers. Acres of trees disappeared. Boulders were shoved aside, hauled away or buried. Roadways were cut. Steep slopes were flattened, ravines filled in. The ancient hillside was redesigned almost overnight.

And all of this was taking place very close to the fox's burrow. A friend who knew of my interest in the fox, a man who knew the hill a bit better than I did, had showed me the den at the end of summer. At the time, he said, the vixen was living there with three pups, having moved there a few weeks earlier from another burrow farther back in the woods.

It was autumn before I had a chance to spy on the fox. I went up there shortly before dusk, found a comfortable log to sit on about 30 yards from the burrow, and waited. A pile of brush—the logging had already begun—screened me from the den, and I felt fairly certain I would finally be able to watch the fox undetected. The only other time I had seen it was during the summer, when I happened upon her as I stepped from the woods into a clearing early one morning. She dashed into the forest in an instant, a red-brown flash, a blur. My look at her probably lasted less than a second, but that was long enough to recognize her, to finally be able to say that I had seen the fox.

My wait in the fading light soon paid off. Less than 20 minutes after the sun had disappeared, I thought I saw some movement at the den, but I couldn't be sure. I don't see too well in darkness; was that the fox or wasn't it? Then I saw a bit of white, and it was moving. Sure, that was her; the tip of a fox's tail is white. As I stared hard, I figured it out. The fox had her head and forelegs down in the hole, her tail flying like a flag above. She seemed to be sealing up the burrow in some manner, or perhaps just giving final instructions to her youngsters before leaving on a hunting trip.

In another few moments, she turned, trotted off the entrance mound into the chest-high grasses and weeds in the clearing, and started circling toward me. When she stopped directly in front of my brush pile, I was sure she had discovered me, but all she did was point her nose straight up into the air, looking for a moment as if she were about to burst into a howl, like a coyote. More likely, though, she was testing the wind, to see what other creatures were around. I was downwind. She didn't notice me. She was beautiful. Even in the poor light, I could see she was sleek and healthy. Her back was a darker color than I expected, but her sides were tawny, and her chest and throat were as white as the tip of her tail. Her eyes and ears were alert, taking in all the sights and sounds of the approaching night. I held my breath; I didn't want to scare her in any way. After all the winter days of tracking foxes on that hill, I finally was watching one. I wanted the moment to last as long as possible.

Quickly, though, she decided on her hunting route, turned and sort of glided through the scrubby meadow toward the woods on the far side. She wasn't running or walking; rather, she was trotting in a gait that made it seem as if she were floating. I saw her swerve into one clump of weeds, then another. Then she was gone.

I went back a couple of other times as fall slipped into winter, but didn't see the fox again. Each time I returned, I noticed there had been more bulldozing up there, and I was becoming convinced the rumbling, ground-shaking monsters had scared off the fox. But I held out hope. Foxes adapt rather well to environmental changes, and few use dens during winter, anyway. They prefer to wander, spending winter days asleep on ledges or beneath low-hanging hemlocks or wherever daylight finds them.

The overnight snow told me I had nothing to worry about—yet. Fox tracks followed all of the lanes and paths on the hill. They roamed across the frozen pond and examined the meadows and most of the rocky ledges. There seemed to be far too many tracks for only one fox. But I found one special set, the one that visited both the burrow near the condo site and the old den in the woods, but apparently entered neither. Maybe she was just checking on her former homes, just remembering the good old days when she had the slope to herself.

I came back from my walk both satisfied that there were still so many tracks and apprehensive about the future. By next winter, there will be people living up there. Will the fox have enough room to roam? I think of following her tracks as good old days, too. I hope this wasn't the last winter for either of us.

75

Last Days of the Monarchs

IF YOU ARE ever to know a woods, do your exploring in winter. When the curtain of leaves is gone, you can more easily examine each ledge and stone wall and pathway. And it's much easier to find the monarchs.

Monarchs are what I call the largest, oldest trees in the forest. In nearly every case, they are left over from the days when the surrounding land was cleared for farming. They were spared from the axe, perhaps to mark a boundary, perhaps to provide shade for livestock or weary farmers. Whatever the reason, they flourished for decades before the younger trees began crowding around again. In summer, the thick growth surging in on all sides obscures their size and majesty. But not now.

Now we can see past the skinny saplings and underbrush. Again, the thick trunks and heavy, horizontal branches of the old trees stand out. None of the younger trees have limbs reaching straight out; there is no room for that in dense forests.

Many of the monarchs are oaks, some are maples, a few are pines or hemlocks or beeches, and a very few are sycamores. They all share similar characteristics—the horizontal branches start low, usually within ten feet of the ground, and they have the strong, regal bearing that comes only from standing alone against the wind and snow and rain for many years. With no competition for sunlight or water, they grew thick and solid, becoming giants that stood guard over the surrounding pastures, hayfields and patches of grain.

Unfortunately, they share another trait, age. Most of these great trees were witnesses to the birth of our nation; they were already tall and strong at the time of the American Revolution. For more than two centuries they have endured, through war and hurricanes, through blizzards and ice storms, through lumbering and land development, through blight and disease, through lightning and drought and pollution and gypsy moths. But now they are facing the one enemy they cannot escape, the years. Many will not survive much longer.

Each year now there are more signs of mortality; a dying branch, a bit of decay, a limb cracking under the weight of snow or ice. Some of the oldest and largest have been deteriorating for several years already. Huge oaks and sycamores, in particular, often have hollow limbs and trunks long before the tree actually dies. Generations of raccoons and squirrels may live in those cavities before the sap rises a final time, before leaves appear for their last spring.

Yet, the trees—especially the monarchs—are able to retain a measure of dignity even after death. As the bark falls off, the bare wood becomes polished by the wind and snow; it takes on a silvery hue when seen against the sky or a backdrop of other trees. The immense trunks and thick limbs appear to be even larger when there are no leaves; the ancient trees loom taller, more stately.

The late author-naturalist Edwin Way Teale once wrote of this afterlife of trees:

"For a great tree, death comes as a gradual transformation. Its vitality ebbs slowly. Even when life has abandoned it entirely, it remains a majestic thing. On some hilltop, a dead tree may dominate the landscape for miles around. Alone among living things, it retains its character and dignity after death. Plants wither; animals disintregate. But a dead tree may be as arresting, as filled with personality, in death as it is in life. Even in its final moments, when the massive trunk lies prone and it has moldered into a ridge covered with mosses and fungi, it arrives at a fitting and a noble end. It enriches and refreshes the earth. And later, as part of other green and growing things, it rises again."

That's true, of course, and if it were not for dead trees there undoubtedly would be a great decline in the cavity-nesting birds—the owls and wood ducks, the chickadees and titmice, the woodpeckers and bluebirds—as well as problems for the raccoons and squirrels. But I still prefer the living trees. I find it reassuring that these giants are standing up to another winter, as they challenged hundreds of winters before, and that they will, indeed, develop more leaves and more acorns or cones or seed capsules when spring and summer return.

Some of the grandest of the old monarchs are no longer with us. Nearly all of the great chestnuts that once loomed over New England are gone. So are most of the finest native elms, which like the chestnuts, fell victim to blight more often than to axes and saws. It is highly unlikely we will ever see monarchs of those species again.

Maybe that's why the "grandfather" oaks and sycamores and hemlocks are so important now. They are the survivors; they have been as solid, as constant, as the rocks and the hills through how many—seven? eight? nine?—generations of New Englanders. From the time of cabins to this age of condominiums, from ox-cart paths to interstates, the mighty trees have always been there.

Now, so many of them are growing weary. Each winter, a few more branches yield to the storms. Each spring, a few more twigs fail to waken to the sunshine. Each summer, a few more saplings crowd closer, stealing a bit of needed nourishment from the monarch's roots. Vitality ebbs.

Some of them still may outlive us. But the largest, the oldest, could be down to their final years. I think of that each time I come across one in the winter woods. So I pause for a moment, and pay my respects.

76

A Possum in the Yard

Other people feed birds or squirrels in the winter. We feed a possum.

It's not by design, but that's the way it has turned out for the last two years. Apparently even animals as, uh, mentally deficient as opossums know a soft touch when they find one.

Actually, it's Rusty's fault. Rusty was the golden retriever that used to rule the backyard as if it were his private fiefdom. When he grew old and slow, however, the other animals started taking advantage of him. First the squirrels and chipmunks moved in, and then the rabbits began making regular raids on the garden. Last winter, the possum made its appearance.

Rusty had long had a habit of not quite finishing his evening meals. No matter what we gave him, or how much, he left a little something in his dish—perhaps planning to come back later for a midnight snack—and leftover food around the yard always attracts attention. Particularly in winter. Other people get stray dogs or cats or foxes or rats sneaking in to check out dog dishes. At our place, it's the possum.

For some time last winter, we weren't sure just what was cleaning up Rusty's leftovers. After the first few light snows, we noticed muddied tracks running to and from the dish. The tracks led to a corner of the yard and under a fence, disappearing beneath a pile of discarded boards and posts. The first thought was rats, and had that been the case, we'd have taken immediate steps to make sure nothing was left in the dish when Rusty was brought inside. We're tolerant of almost anything, but not rats.

By the time there was good tracking snow, however, it was obvious we were dealing with something larger than a rat. But the tracks were not familiar. So we put the boys' Hav-a-Hart trap out there one night. That's a box-shaped wire contraption that catches unwary animals without hurting them. My sons used it in the past to see if they could outsmart the squirrels that constantly loot the bird feeder. They did, once or twice, but squirrels catch on pretty quickly.

Possums are not that bright. The first night we set the trap, baiting it with dog food, we had the possum by eight o'clock. We released it, watched it waddle off to its pile of boards and then reset the trap. By nine o'clock, we had caught it again. And the next night, it walked into the box a third time. After that, we put the trap away.

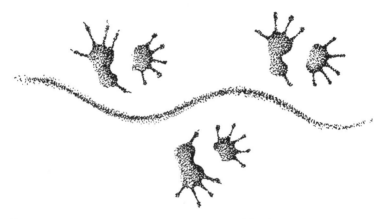

Ever see a possum in winter? No animal looks more out of place, more miserable, than a possum plodding through the snow. And it is out of place. They were once Southern critters, seldom seen above the Mason-Dixon line. For some reason, they started coming North, and now are fairly common in New England.

But they're certainly not equipped for our winters. Their tails are hairless, their ears and feet are bare. They have fur, but it's so thin it looks threadbare, and their faces have very little protection. It's not unusual for possums to suffer frostbite.

They can look pretty sorry in cold weather. As a Connecticut naturalist once wrote about a possum he saw, "It looked like a youngster lost in a storm, tears in its eyes and its nose red and running."

Last spring we disposed of the boards and posts, and found no trace of the possum. Apparently it had already moved to its summer quarters. I have no idea where those are—we didn't see a sign of possums for months—and I forgot about last winter's freeloader until one day recently when I was stocking the bird feeder. I began wondering if the possum was still around, and how such a pathetic creature would survive without us.

So I put out a little dog food, just as an experiment, as soon as there was snow. Sure enough, the next morning the food was gone and the possum's tracks were there, leading to a hole beneath the garden shed.

I seriously doubt the possum has been there all this time—Rusty has been gone for months, his dish has been empty—but I'm just as sure no possum is smart enough to remember that it found good things to eat there last winter. So I don't know how to explain what has happened unless this is a different possum, which just wandered by at the right time.

Now I have to decide whether to continue feeding it. I find it hard to simply ignore something that seems so helpless. I don't think Rusty would approve, but his dish just may have a new use for the rest of the winter.

77

Invisible Visitors

OUR INVISIBLE NEIGHBORS are still around. Or perhaps they went away and just recently returned. It's hard to say for certain when you are dealing with invisible creatures.

They are quail, the chunky little game birds that some people call bobwhites. They are so secretive there are only a couple of times a year when I know for sure that they are still nearby. One is in early summer, when their clear, cheery whistles ring out from the edges of the meadows and woods. *Bob-WHITE! Bob-bob-WHITE!* The other time is when they leave footprints in snow.

We almost never see the birds. I remember flushing four of them one fall when I stopped at a sumac thicket to snip off a few of the crimson plumes. Another time, at dawn, I saw a lone quail scratching around in the dirt in the meadow, looking just like a chicken in a barnyard. And there were a couple of times, several winters ago, when a small covey would come out to the cracked corn we scattered around the cedars above the swamp.

Most of the time, though, they remain invisible. I suppose I could find them even now if I went crashing around out there. I have a pretty good idea of where they like to spend the winter. They congregate in one place when there is snow and use another area when the ground is bare. Sooner or later I would come close to stepping on them and they'd fly up, exploding from their hiding places all at the same time. But I would be defeating myself. Too much disturbance and they'll simply move out.

Earlier this winter, we again tried to lure the quail into view with cracked corn, but it didn't work very well. The corn lured too many other creatures. Ten minutes after we spread the corn, the area beneath the cedars was covered with doves and cardinals and sparrows and starlings. Sometimes pigeons and crows stopped by as well. Once, a herring gull landed there; it looked as out of place as quail would be on a beach. When the squirrels discovered the corn, we gave up. Squirrels get enough free meals from us at the feeders in the yard.

But I know the quail are still out there. It's been a long time since I've seen one, and the last *Bob-WHITE* whistle I heard must have been at least six months ago, but even invisible birds cannot walk in snow without leaving tracks. A day after a recent snowfall I went looking and found the tracks at the edge of the woods. Right where they belong.

Quail are something special to me. They were among the first birds I became interested in as a kid. We didn't have many colorful songbirds around our farm, and those we did have—meadowlarks, red-winged blackbirds, robins—were too common to be exciting. But there were quail in the hayfields and the pastures and the woods, and I found their whistling at courtship time intriguing.

I didn't see quail often in those days, either, but I remember noticing how perky, almost jaunty, they always seemed to be, whether they were chasing grasshoppers or pecking at fallen apples in our orchard. I liked the bright eyes and stripes on the head, the males' white throats and rakish crests. They may be basically red-brown ground birds that blend in with their surroundings, but they struck me as particularly handsome. They still do.

Over the years, I've gotten to know quail only slightly better. I doubt if I've found half a dozen nests, and only two or three times have I found a "quail ring" in the snow. At night, a covey of quail will form a circle on the ground, heads facing outward and bodies touching, for both protection and warmth. They'll remain in this position in a snowfall and the entire circle may be covered by morning. Usually, though, unless it's a heavily crusted snow, the birds can break out when hungry enough, leaving behind the unique ring.

One thing I haven't learned about quail is why a flock is called a covey—I know of no other birds that travel in coveys—but I guess that's not important.

What is important is that there are still a few quail around. It's good to know there are a few out there in the snow, that there will probably be some more whistles for us to look forward to next spring. I'm so glad they're still in the neighborhood I don't even mind if they remain invisible.

78

Old Barns

THE BEAMS ARE HUGE, each one hacked and hewn from oak logs. The joints are fitted with precision, and held together with long oak pegs. The walls and roof are covered with ancient wooden shingles, nailed there generations ago.

Old barns, even those no longer used, are never empty. They are filled with character.

I like barns. Particularly big, old wooden barns. When visiting farms, I always spend more time poking around the barn than checking out the house. But there aren't many really old barns around anymore. Even those built by skilled craftsmen are feeling the weight of the decades; a few more crumble or are torn down each year. They are becoming an endangered species.

And that's sad. New England barns are unique. Not only were the old ones built with simple hand tools—can you imagine fashioning even one beam using only an ax and an adze?—but each was a little different. They were designed on the spot, shaped to fit both the needs of the individual farmer and the lay of the land. Many were built right into hillsides. Those are my favorites.

Eric Sloane, who spent years studying the early days of this country, wrote in one of his books: "It might be said that the early barn is the best example of American colonial architecture. Each old barn was born of American soil and fitted to an American landscape for specific American needs. The early American home was varied in planning but generally European in design. The barns in Europe were small, just big enough to house a few horses or cattle, but when they built an American

barn, it became the symbol of a new life. From the beginning the American barn was big, like the hopes and plans for life in the New World. It was unlike anything built anywhere else. It was entirely American."

The craftsmanship that went into the barns varied, of course, as much as the designs. Barns that were built by talented, trained hands remain solid, defying the years. Those that were put up hastily are sagging, ready to tumble, losing their dignity and character along with their shape and form.

Barns that were built into a hillside were done so for good reason. Most faced south, the direction of optimum sunshine and warmth, and let the hill protect them from the sharp north wind. Also, set on a slope, the barn could easily have two floors at "ground level." Livestock would use the bottom, entering from the slope's lower side, while the second floor would be just as accessible from the hilltop. That way, harvest could be hauled directly to the loft, an arrangement I envy when I remember all the strenuous pitching of hay my brothers and I had to do in our high Midwestern barn.

I'm not sure what I find so fascinating about old barns. Part of it, though, is the architecture. I particularly like barns with a cupola or two on top. Cupolas indicate that the farmer cared about the building—the barn was more than just a place to put animals.

Part of it is the history. These barns were here long before tractors and electricity and refrigeration and computers. They stand as a symbol of what can be done—what was done—by human minds and muscles and sweat.

And some of my fascination may come from a kinship I like to think I have with the men and women who labored in these barns, feeding and watering cows every day, milking them each morning and evening. I did that, too, in almost the same manner—no automatic milkers or electric pumps for us. Maybe that's why I feel at home in old barns.

I walk into an old barn now, even one that has been abandoned for years, and it all comes back. The fragrance of dry hay is poignant. Lying around are fragments of early farming life—a milking stool, baling twine, nail kegs, pitchfork handles, even mice-chewed bits of harnesses. It takes only a minute, and a pleasant plunge into imagination, for me to see the billowing breath clouds of the cows on winter mornings, for me to hear the horses snorting and stamping in their stalls.

Southern New England's barns have been vanishing for years. One by one, as farmers pulled out or sold out, the buildings disappeared. There are not many left.

Now it's happening in northern New England, too. On a recent drive through New Hampshire and Vermont, I counted dozens of abandoned and forgotten farms. Already, most of the outbuildings are gone—the spring house, icehouse, woodshed, blacksmith shop, carriage shed, chicken coop. In most cases, even the house is gone. Only the barn remains, but it won't much longer.

That is disturbing. Barns are as much a part of the New England heritage as gabled houses and white churches and covered bridges. They may not be important to some of us, but as long as people farm—which will be as long as people eat—we'll owe something to what these barns represent. Such monuments shouldn't be allowed to rot away.

79

Mouse Tunnels

THE SUBWAY BUILDERS have been at it again. In the right conditions, their tunnels are easy to find. They're on top of the ground.

These tunnels are in snow, and the diggers are field mice and their relatives, the shrews and voles. All it takes is an inch or two of snow, and they go to work. Not even skiers love snow as much as these little critters. Snow makes their lives so much easier: it provides both warmth and protection as they seek new food sources.

Mice don't really have a very easy time of it, especially in winter. They are at the top of nearly every predator's list of favorite foods. Hawks eat more mice than anything else. So do foxes, and owls, and weasels, and stray cats, and probably half a dozen other hunters— when nothing else is available, there are always mice. No wonder they are so nervous. If I had that many monsters chasing me, I'd be a little paranoid, too.

The tunnels help a great deal. And it is amazing how many the mice build. When the snow melts down to the last inch or so, the tunnels are revealed; look for them in meadows or weedy places, like roadsides and edges of the woods. Every winter, it seems, I find more of them. I'm not sure if that means there are more mice or I simply notice things like that more, but these days I seem to come across the tunnels nearly everywhere I walk.

Not long ago, I wandered along the edge of a field that bordered a small stream. There had been a slight thaw a few days earlier, just enough to uncover the tunnels. There were scores of them—a virtual maze— extending from the weeds and tall grass by the brook. The trails wandered out into the field, 15 or 20 or 25 feet, before ending, probably

where the snow had been swept away by the wind. The mice or shrews or voles evidently had been feeding on the grasses and seeds in the field, or were exploring areas too risky for them to visit at any other time.

Perhaps mice go into that field in summer, too, but there is a good chance that those that venture out there in the barrenness of winter, even at night, do not make it back. There are too many eyes and noses, talons and teeth, always searching for mice. That's why the mice need snow and tunnels.

The best snow for these tunnel builders is a soft one (for easy digging) that is quickly capped by an ice crust. Even in two inches of snow, a mouse inside its tunnel is invisible to the sharp-eyed owls and hawks. Add a crust on the snow surface, and the safety margin becomes even greater. Then, even the keen-nosed foxes have more trouble. They may still be able to locate the mice, but the extra moment that it takes a fox to paw or plunge through the crust is usually all it takes for a mouse to escape.

There's warmth, too, inside the snowbanks. The winds may howl outside, and temperatures fall below zero, but the mouse in the snow tunnel won't know it. It will be snug and well fed, and relatively safe, until the next thaw.

Of course, many mice, shrews and voles won't survive winter, whether they are in tunnels or not. They aren't meant to; the laws of Nature require that they provide sustenance for the predators. That's their assigned role. Without mice, the hawks and owls and foxes might disappear.

But there is no need to feel sorry for the mice. They are in no danger of extinction. There may not be a more common mammal in New England than the field mouse. Every meadow has dozens of them; perhaps hundreds. Every mouse that is killed in winter is replaced in spring. In fact, it often becomes a case of there not being enough predators to keep the mouse population in check, rather than too many of the mice being devoured.

Even knowing that, and having no particular affinity for mice in general, I still get a good feeling when looking over their winter handiwork. I'm not sure why. Maybe I consider mice the underdogs, because their enemies are so much larger. Maybe it's because there are so many different creatures after each mouse—I wonder how many times a mouse has dashed away from a fox right into the clutches of an owl. Maybe it's because there is a hint of genius in the network of tunnels.

Whatever the reason, I find a small measure of satisfaction in the tunnels. It's as if they somehow even up the odds a bit. If I had to choose, I'd still rather have an owl around than a mouse, but maybe because of the tunnels there is no reason to choose. We can continue to have both. That, obviously, is the way it all was designed.

80

Seeing the Wind

SNOWDRIFTS ARE USUALLY TROUBLE. They so often appear just where big piles of snow are not wanted—in front of doors and across driveways and over roads. But there can be a good side to the drifts, too. They allow us to see the wind.

When they appear where they don't have to be shoveled away or driven through, drifts can be downright beautiful. They are the immaculate sculptured record of the wind's path, all of its swirls and curls and twists captured in smooth, graceful lines. If there is such a thing as frozen motion, it is the snowdrifts.

There are a few other times when the wind becomes visible, or more accurately, times when we can see its routes. Sand dunes are shaped by wind, although not in the fine detail of snowdrifts, and autumn leaves are tossed around by gusts of wind. A strong wind, however, can cause leaves to drift, too. Last fall, such a wind swept my front lawn clean, but neatly deposited all the leaves in a windrow two feet high on the east side of the house.

Most dramatically, though, the wind makes its mark in snow.

Wind is the one natural element that can rule all the others. Snow without wind is seldom a problem in this part of the world; add wind, though, and we can have a killer of a blizzard. Hurricanes and tornadoes are wind whipped up to fantastic—and deadly—strengths. A serene lake turns dangerous when wind creates whitecaps. Even fire can usually be tamed until wind grabs it and takes it for one of its wild rides. Wind makes all the difference.

At this time of year, wind is a force to be reckoned with every day.

Just as we say in summer that it's not the heat, it's the humidity, now we say it's not the temperature, it's the wind chill. A 10- or 15-degree day is not so hard to deal with when the sun is shining and the air is still. But turn up the wind velocity to 20 or 25 knots and it becomes big trouble. Frostbite and worse become real possibilities.

Television weather forecasters love to show the routes of winter wind. These frigid blasts, say the meteorologists, usually sweep down from Canada, gathering strength as they go. One might be called an Alberta Clipper, another a Siberian Express. But they are all the same in the one respect that matters: they're cold. Painfully cold. Cold enough to sting the skin and bring tears to the eyes. Cold enough to reach down into lungs and steal breath away.

Cold enough to keep me indoors.

Such wind, particularly on winter nights, has a special voice. It whines across the open yard and howls around the corners of the house. It rattles the doors and windows, like some enraged beast trying to get inside. When I'm sitting in front of the fireplace, I can hear it wailing high in the chimney, skirmishing with the heat in some sort of confrontation as old as the earth. The cavemen, I'm certain, listened to the same invisible battles.

When there is fresh snow, the wind leaves behind its tracks, just as surely as the fox's footprints on the hill show where it has roamed in the darkness. If the wind has moved on by morning, I go out looking. When there is enough snow, I can count on deep drifts with graceful contours, and often overhanging lips, around each building. I can see how the wind crashed into the walls, and then bounced off and rushed around the corners. I can see how it divided around tree trunks and fence posts, and then flowed back into a solid force as it swept across the yard.

If the snowfall is light, the drifts are smaller, but more numerous. Then, little piles stretch away from each sapling, each rock, each weed stem in the meadow. These miniature drifts are often delicate, almost feathery, and maybe even more detailed than the monsters left by blizzards. They show exactly where the wind raced on its charge across the land.

And the tiny drifts have something else going for them. They don't make me get out the shovel.

81

Bettie vs. The Squirrels

THE WAR RAGES ON, but the momentum has shifted. I think the squirrels are winning.

My wife, Bettie, is getting desperate. No matter what we do, squirrels continue getting into her bird feeders. And they are so darned arrogant about it.

We've had problems with squirrels in other winters, but never to this degree. I know it's because we no longer have a dog roaming around the yard. Rusty may never have caught one of the squirrels, but he was enough of a threat that they kept their raids to a minimum. He sometimes treed them for hours. Now they act as if it's their divine right to live off our sunflower seeds and cracked corn.

The invasions have come from two areas.

Squirrels cross the street to hit the plastic feeder on our living room window, and other squirrels come from the cedars in a little swamp to get at the big box feeder in the backyard. Bettie doesn't want them at either place, so she has declared war.

Yes, she knows there are so-called squirrel-proof feeders on the market, but there is a principle of sorts involved here. It's become a challenge, a battle of wills.

The plastic hopper is meant for tiny birds—chickadees, finches, juncos, titmice—but the squirrels don't care. They found it and became bolder each day. At first, they simply jumped up, grabbed a mouthful of seeds from the bottom of the hopper, and left. Then they began taking their time, gazing into the house between bites. Bettie banged on the glass so hard a few times I expected her to break the window. It didn't help.

When a squirrel jumped up on the window sill and then flipped open the plastic feeder to stuff himself, she took more drastic action. First, she taped the lid down. When that didn't work—a squirrel chewed through the tape—she had one of our sons fashion a wire screen to put inside the lid, but that didn't stop the squirrels even for a day. They simply pulled the screen out and threw it into a shrub.

The backyard battle hasn't gone much better. At Bettie's insistence, I closed one side of the big screened-in box completely and narrowed the openings on the other side with a board that covered the bottom half of the holes. In less than a day a squirrel chewed through the board and reopened one of the holes.

So I suggested moving the box. We took it off the wooden pole—too easy to climb—and roped it onto the metal bars of the kids' old jungle gym. It still was close enough to the trees for squirrels to jump onto the feeder, but at least we'd make things a little more difficult.

That's what we thought. About two hours after we moved the box, I saw a squirrel come into the yard, climb up the old wooden post, and sit for a moment where the box had been. It looked bewildered, and I was kind of smug. Thought we had it fooled.

Wrong! It was simply angry. It jumped down, went to the maple, climbed up to a branch near a swinging tin can that we fill with sunflower seeds, grasped the can with both front paws and emphatically turned it over, dumping out every single seed. I expected the squirrel to turn toward me and say, "Take that!"

Then it ran along the stack of firewood, looked up at the box now on the gym set, and hesitated only a moment. Instead of going into the tree and leaping down, as I expected, the squirrel jumped to the ground and immediately scampered up the steel post of the gym set as easily as it climbed the old wooden pole. I was amazed.

Later I put bars, in the form of long spikes, beside the entrance holes, once more making the box squirrel-proof. That, too, was successful only temporarily. After sitting on the roof and cussing us out, the squirrels went back to gnawing. By the second day they had chewed the wood beneath the holes so much that the spikes pulled loose.

We're thinking now of suspending the box from the boys' basketball rim. That's set on steel poles, too, and it is farther from the trees. But I'm not too confident. By now, the squirrels are as determined as we are. I suggested to Bettie that maybe she ought to just give up the fight and feed squirrels instead of birds for the rest of the winter. Her answer might have burned their ears.

82

Ice in the Marsh

ONE WINTER IT was a huge muskrat lodge hidden back in a dense stand of cattails. Another time, I found half a dozen old red-winged blackbird nests taken over by deermice, which had crammed the nests with seeds and dried berries. This year, I found the caddisflies.

Big discoveries? Of course not. But they are interesting, and all were made possible by ice. It is only when ice comes that I can really poke around the little marshes and backwater pools, places that are barred to me the rest of the year. The water is too shallow and the channels through the weeds too narrow for the canoe, and the muddy bottoms too soft for wading, so I can only look from shore until the ice comes.

Usually, though, by this time of winter I can roam about freely. Ice-fishermen and skaters and hockey players have their own reasons for welcoming thick ice; for me, it means a chance to do some exploring.

In spring, summer and autumn, a marsh or small pond is lively, as busy a place as there is for wild creatures, whether they be birds or insects or plants. Something is always happening.

But in winter, a marsh seems to be the most barren, most desolate part of the countryside. There are none of the bird sounds you might find around the yard, none of the rabbit and squirrel tracks of the woods edges, not even the vibrant colors of the hemlock and pine groves. In the marsh, there are no obvious signs of life. The cattail stalks are brown, broken and forlorn. The lily pads are deathly black and limp. There are no sounds, except for the whistling wind, and no motion, except for weeds and reeds whipped about by that relentless wind.

Yet, there is life there. Hidden life and dormant life and suspended life. For some creatures, winter takes them very close to death. For some others, the freeze-up, the coming of ice, is a blessing.

Now, when I can walk the narrow, twisting channels in the cattails, I look for muskrat lodges. Nearly every pond has them, sometimes beaver-style mounds of sticks and mud, sometimes smaller lodges of reeds and stalks. Frequently, the lodges can be seen from shore, but one of the largest I found was far back in a maze of cattails, a huge lodge about six feet across, made almost entirely of cattail stalks. It was low, and frozen solid, and totally concealed from the banks. If it hadn't been for the ice, I never would have found it. Chances are, the muskrats' enemies probably find the lodges, too, when ice is in, but by then the lodge is a frozen fortress, and the muskrats no longer have to worry about being discovered. Down below, they are safe and comfortable, and as long as they can swim about freely, they're in little danger of running out of food. It always seems the first few I see when ice goes out are plenty sleek; winter is not a particularly hard time for muskrats.

It can be more difficult for something like deermice, but they prepare themselves well. Take, for example, the mouse or mice that converted

the blackbird nests into storage bins. The nests were low, just above the water line, in small bushes. Yet, each of the six nests in the red-wings' colony was filled to overflowing with weed seeds and berries of a wide variety. Those bushes are never out of the water, and until there is ice a deermouse or any other animal would have to swim 10 to 15 feet out from shore. Yet, the nests appear to have been stocked months ago, well before ice arrived. Would the mice really do that, swim out there, just to store their goodies? It's the kind of "mystery" I like, another of the fringe benefits of ice.

Henry David Thoreau wrote that he often would lie on the ice of Walden Pond and watch the happenings in the water below. That's a good way to get cold, but it's also a way to see things a walker might miss.

Like the caddisflies. They are strange creatures indeed. Not only do the larvae build their own portable shelters and the adults never eat a bite, but they frequently are active in February, below the ice, when most self-respecting insects are still contentedly snoozing away the winter.

Caddisflies are one form of insect much more interesting as larvae than adults. In fact, I seldom even notice the adults. Apparently, they live only briefly in the adult stage—just long enough to mate and lay eggs, I suppose—and never eat at all. Not much to look forward to, is it? But they may live a full year as larvae, crawling around the submerged weeds and rocks in the ponds and swamps.

Their best features, of course, are the little shelters each one builds and carries along. Some are made of sand cemented together, some are tubes made of tiny leaves, and others—my favorites—are tiny, rectangular twig enclosures, miniature log cabins.

I'm never sure which caddisfly does what, since there are more than 1,000 species in North America. There are even some that spin silken nets that they attach to rocks in fast-flowing streams to catch prey. Smart creatures, the caddisflies.

But, if they're so smart, why are they crawling around in that frigid water now? If they get caught in the ice, they won't make it to spring. Not even inside their log cabins.

83

The Beach in Winter

THE NAMES ARE unfamiliar but intriguing. Scoters and eiders. Harlequins and brant. Bluebills and goldeneyes. They're all sea birds— ducks and geese—and winter is the best time to see them. But, in reality, they are excuses.

We say the birds are the reason Bettie and I spend more time at the ocean in winter than in summer, but I always end up admiring the sea as much as the birds. There is something about the ocean in winter, when all the fury and might of the waves are unleashed, that I find irresistible. Give me a stormy February day along a breakwater, and you can keep all the 90-degree afternoons on sandy beaches.

The ocean takes on another dimension in winter storms. What is wilder, more primitive, more awesome than immense waves crashing ashore? Watch the white foam spraying high above the rocks. Before one wave has a chance to dissipate and drain back, hissing and foaming, to the sea, another explodes on top of it. The waves are only water; the ocean has no emotion. But it's hard to stand beside the churning, roiling, seething breakers and not think of the sea as angry. The waves slam ashore so hard, so relentlessly, you get the idea that the sea is trying to reassert itself, to reinforce its claim as the earth's oldest and most powerful force.

Just as imposing as the sights are the sounds. Listen to the booming reverberations of the endless waves, mixed with the roar of the wind and the cries of the gulls, and it's as if you are hearing the world at its creation. The sound of the sea is the sound of the ages. You may be sitting in your car, within a few yards of lavish houses or condominiums, but the sounds

are of an untamed and untamable place far beyond man's domination. The sea remains wild and free.

The birds make their own contributions to the elemental wildness of the scene. Gulls, of course, are the most visible and certainly the noisiest, but they are so common I tend to look past them. Except for the big black-backed gulls, all gulls look alike to me. As far as I'm concerned, they're all herring gulls—the same birds we have all summer—and hardly worth a second glance. Real birders can spot several other gulls, but I couldn't tell a Bonaparte's gull from an Icelandic gull, so I seldom bother trying.

Scoters are much more interesting. They are wandering ducks that seem to enjoy the ocean most when it is roughest. Usually we see them in flocks, bobbing around in the mountainous swells as calmly as mallards floating on a millpond. Often the scoters venture so near the rocks I keep expecting the next wave to smash them to bits, but it never seems to happen. They just like to live dangerously, I guess.

Eiders and harlequins are colorful, rather exotic ducks from the Far North that winter off our coast. They and another species with a picturesque name, the old-squaw, are harder to find than scoters, but occasionally come close to shore in stormy times. Seeing them can make our day.

Brant are big, dark geese that show up in flocks, if they show up at all. Bluebills (scaup) and goldeneyes are rather common winter ducks. Even casual birders can find them. It's the same with the various kinds of mergansers, including the attractive little hooded mergansers that are among my favorite water birds. Grebes and loons are out there, too, resting and feeding, awaiting the signal to head back north for the breeding season.

So there are usually plenty of birds to make winter visits to the coast interesting. But every so often, we'll drive down there and see little other than gulls. Maybe the wind isn't quite right, or the birds are too far offshore. They can't always be counted on.

Still, it doesn't seem to matter all that much whether we find one flock of scoters or a thousand mergansers. The ocean is always there, and yet different, new, every time. In winter, the sea and the waves can be both intimidating and inspiring. Frightening and mesmerizing. Violent and strangely comforting. And forever fascinating. In winter, I cannot stay away.

84

Close to the Stars

THE COLD IS BITING, but it doesn't matter that much. After all, the night is calling. Every so often, it seems, I have to get out there, to walk in the night, to walk with the stars.

On these winter-night walks I usually start out looking for foxes or owls or other creatures that reserve most of their activity for the darkness. Invariably, however, I end up spending most of my time gazing at the sky. In winter, the stars are too bright, too close, too comforting, to be ignored.

Perhaps, in their own ways, the stars and constellations of the other seasons are just as interesting, but I couldn't say—I never notice. The sky just isn't as clear at other times of the year, and warm weather too often means mosquitoes. It's hard to appreciate the sky while swatting those blasted little pests.

Tonight, I head for a high hill, without even thinking why. I climb around up there often, so it might be from habit, but there might also be a subconscious reason for going up there: on certain winter nights, the stars look so close it seems I could reach up and touch them, if I could just get a little higher. Of course it's nonsense, but on a cold, clear, still winter night, the impossible seems merely difficult.

As I walk, another advantage of night wandering in winter becomes apparent. There is no need for a flashlight. Even without a moon, it's not really dark out. The snow creates a soft luminescence, providing enough light that I soon leave my familiar trail and climb toward a rocky knoll that my family calls Sassafras Ledge. I'd never attempt to scale that steep slope, covered as it is with logs and rocks, in summer darkness; tonight,

I can see well enough that I twice pause to look over fox tracks.

From the ledge, I turn and look out over the valley and the village beyond. A frozen pond below lies smooth, white and unmarked, like a space left blank in the center of a pencil drawing. The village—which, because of the lights, always seems larger at night than during the day— also appears considerably larger in winter than in summer, when leaves

hide many of the lights. Now, each street is outlined in lights. More light glows through house and shop windows. It's a lovely sight; I wonder how many in the village have ever seen it from this perspective.

I wander off through the woods, thinking again how things change at night. At this time it's a black-and-white world, with a few touches of gray.

The pines and hemlock, vibrant green during the day, now stand dark and foreboding.

There is almost no sound. I hear an old tree creak and groan, and there is a faint murmur high in the pines from some light breeze that I can't even feel. I listen intently for an owl, but hear none. The loudest noise comes from my own footsteps in the snow.

At the very top of the hill, I linger, my eyes drawn to the sky. Uncountable stars are up there, and while I still can't touch them, I marvel at their clarity and brilliance. Again, as every winter, I notice that some have definite blue or red hues. I never see that in the summer stars.

As always, Orion is my point of reference when I try to identify constellations. The bright three-star line that the ancients saw as making up a hunter's belt is an old friend. I remember, during the winters when my job required leaving the house at 2:30 a.m., I would glance up as I stepped outside. Orion would be there, ever faithful, and that somehow assured me that at least something was still right with the world.

I don't know many constellations, and my comprehension fails at times even with those I should know. The old Greeks and Romans who made them up had imaginations far more vivid than mine.

But I can find Orion's neighbors in the sky, the triangular formation that represents Taurus the bull and the group of tiny stars known as the Seven Sisters of the Pleiades. That's another of my favorite constellations, probably because those stars are so far away —more than 400 light-years—and it takes particularly clear nights like this for me to see them.

Nearly two hours slide by before I return to the house. Some of the lights have blinked off in the village. I haven't heard an owl or seen a fox yet. But Orion is still up there, leading the chase across the sky. There is still something fundamentally, and eternally, right with the world.

85

Half-past February

I̶T DOESN'T ALWAYS turn out that way, but once we've reached half-past February, once we've passed the middle of this month, I feel we're over the ridge. It should be all downhill from here. We're going to make it to spring, after all.

Half-past February. This is the time when almost anything can happen. We could be finding the first sprouts of skunk cabbage poking up in the marsh one day, and then be buried by a blizzard the next. Quite often, in fact, our biggest storms of winter come in the second half of February. But by now there is a difference: these lapses back into snow and ice and cold are only temporary—we can feel it, sense it, actually believe it.

The difference is mainly in the staying power of the snow. Almost as soon as a storm peters out in mid-February, the snow starts melting. Sunshine, coming from a higher angle than earlier, now has a real effect on the snow. A month ago, it merely bounced off the drifts.

This is icicle time. A month ago, if there were long icicles hanging from the eaves it meant the house was poorly insulated; too much heat was going up to the roof. Now, there are dripping icicles on nearly every building, nearly every day. The air may seem no warmer than at Christmas, but the change is there—the higher arc of the sun is doing its thing.

It's also the time for sap-cicles. Gradually, inevitably, sap begins to rise in the trees at half-past February. Most years, it's too early to start tapping the maples until at least Washington's Birthday, but the sap rise is already evident; just look at the reddening in the twigs. Often now,

when maple twigs and branches are broken, the sap bleeds from the wounds, and freezes. The results are the slightly sweet ice daggers that become the first lessons for so many children in what sap really is.

I've been in New England long enough now that I shouldn't expect early springs. In the area where I grew up, in the Midwest, my brothers and I would start throwing baseballs by half-past February; by the first of March, we figured winter was all through. Red-winged blackbirds would be arriving in huge flocks. We'd see the first woodchucks (we called them groundhogs) and first chipmunks.

But old habits aren't cast aside easily. Even though I know better, every year I start looking for signs of spring too early. The first time I hear a brook trickling down the hillside I go looking for migrating ducks—and find the ponds still locked in ice. Redwings, and swallows, too, never show up here as early as I think they should. I've never seen a woodchuck before mid-March here—usually, it's not until April—but I still start checking their dens every February.

Yet there are the signs, subtle as they are, that we may indeed be over the ridge. Dawn comes noticeably earlier now. Along with the sap rise in the maples, we can see amber glows in the willow tips, and the reddening of numerous bog-land bushes. Jays and chickadees have new, somewhat jaunty notes in their voices.

In reality, winter has a considerable way to go. The rest of it may be downhill, but the slope is long and occasionally treacherous: two more weeks of February, and then the cruel tease that is March. The ride is never smooth. We slide into snowbanks and shiver in icy rain and get buffeted by cutting gales. March here may not be real winter, but it certainly cannot be called spring.

So I try not to get too excited about reaching half-past February. The seasons simply cannot be rushed. Redwings and swallows won't be here tomorrow, or the day after, or next week.

But the birds—and spring—are coming. The sap is rising. Life is stirring down in the roots and twigs and buds. The progress is slow and deliberate, but as sure as anything on this planet. Somehow, just knowing that will make these final weeks of winter a little easier to take.

86

Beaver Ponds

SEVERAL SMALL STUMPS stand along the edge of the pond, each with a conical top, each with a scattering of wood chips on the ground. Some of the larger trees that were cut down are now just decaying logs, partially chewed, often to the core. Trees from other stumps are gone entirely.

Farther out in the pond, a pile of brush smeared with frozen mud looms large and silent, locked in ice. Numerous sticks and branches show through the ice, most of them yellow-white, obviously stripped of their bark.

For years, it seems, I've been waiting for this: a chance to really examine a beaver pond. Beavers may be nothing more than overgrown rodents to some people, but to me they are something special. They are a link with the mountain men and the trappers and the early explorers of North America. They are wildness and wilderness. They are what this country was before "civilization" came to level the forests and dam the rivers and pollute the streams and cover the countryside with farms and houses and factories.

Beavers vanished from Rhode Island 200 years ago. Perhaps before that. Now a few of them have returned.

It's not as it was, and never again will be; but just having a few beavers around is better than having none.

Beavers have been slowly and steadily increasing for the past several years, many overflowing into Rhode Island from a Connecticut restoration program. A story assignment on beavers last fall put me in contact with some of the state wildlife experts, and they clued me in on where to find the ponds. I have been waiting for adequate ice in order to get a firsthand look at the animals' work.

Seeing beavers is not easy. Besides being active almost exclusively at night, they are extremely wary of people. Most of the time, the closest you can get to a beaver is hearing a loud *whack!* as one of the critters smacks its tail on the water, warning the others of an intruder. I suppose if you sat all night at the edge of a pond, remaining perfectly still, and there was enough moonlight, you might glimpse a beaver or two. Maybe.

The next best thing is finding all the signs of their presence; and with beavers, there are more signs than with other animals. Often, the first indication that they are around is the rising level in a pond, or the abrupt change in a stream. Both indicate that beavers have built a dam, their trademark. Whether 100 feet long and elaborate or merely a handful of sticks jammed into a culvert, the dams are meant to create or deepen ponds. Beavers need deep ponds in winter in order to have enough water beneath the ice for swimming and for storing their food. They also have to be able to enter and leave their lodges without venturing into the open. So they build dams. They don't care if roads and fields are flooded in the process—they were here first, after all—and people who try tearing down the dams soon learn how persistent beavers can be about their chosen places. If necessary, they'll rebuild a dam night after night.

Some of the beaver signs can be looked at from shore: the stumps, the trails from the water to an aspen or poplar grove, the short sticks stripped bare of all bark. But to examine the lodge, ice is almost a necessity. With the pond surface frozen solid, you won't get to hear the beaver's tail-slap warning but you can walk right up to his house.

The lodges are surprisingly large, often extending four or five feet above the water level, and stretching well over a dozen feet in diameter. The entrances—at least two of them—are under water (and therefore beneath the ice), but they lead to a roomy and dry chamber in the center

of the pile of sticks, above the water line. Now that the mud-caked walls are frozen, the lodge is close to being a solid fortress. If you look carefully, though, at the top of the lodge, you can see an area of sticks not plastered in mud. The beavers were smart enough to leave these air holes, and when it's cold you can see the frost rings formed by their breath freezing on the outer lodge branches.

Because they worked so hard last fall in cutting down saplings and towing them to caches in the water, the beavers now can dine contentedly all winter without venturing beyond their shield of ice. Those saplings were jammed into the mud on the pond's bottom, and now, when the ice is clear, it's easy to look through it at those branches already used and discarded. Beavers feed mainly on bark, and when they've stripped all the bark from one sapling they move on to the next. The discarded stick then floats free, resting just beneath the ice cover. If the ice remains for another month, the beavers may get hungry enough to return to that branch and gnaw some more. It will still be there, well preserved in the beavers' own form of deep freeze.

There was a time, years ago, when I spent my winter mornings and evenings running a trap line. I know trapping is frowned upon these days, but at that time, in that part of the country, it was a way of life—one of the few ways a farm boy could earn money in winter.

I caught muskrats and raccoons, mostly. Those kids luckier, or more skilled, caught a mink once in a while. That was the ultimate in our area. But we talked a lot about beaver, about what it must have been like when Jim Bridger and Kit Carson and the other mountain men made their living by trapping beaver. My lowly muskrat line gave me a closer feeling of kinship with the old-timers than anything else I did—fishing, hunting, chopping trees, plowing new ground, anything. Maybe trapping just seemed more glamorous, the wandering through the valleys and over hills so adventurous.

But muskrats were not beavers. To me, a beaver was an animal of legend, something from the history books, about as real as a dinosaur.

That's why it's so enjoyable now to go just a few miles and find half a dozen ponds with dams and lodges and the telltale stumps. But I certainly wouldn't try trapping the beaver, even if it became legal. Not only do I find living animals more intriguing than dead ones, but it's important that future generations of imaginative boys get this chance to see a real beaver pond. I'm glad they won't have to wait as long as I did.

87

Skunk Cabbage

By THE LAST week of February, I start looking for signs. Winter has to end sometime; maybe this year spring will be early. So I head for the bog—skunk cabbage never lets me down.

Some years, there are many signs by now. The fuzzy, silvery catkins on the pussy willows may be open and shining. Bushes along the stream may have reddening twigs as they snap out of winter's dormancy. Sap could be rising already in the maples; in fact, this is traditionally the week when sugar makers start tapping the maples and turning that sap into syrup.

There can be other signs, too. When March is on the horizon, it seems time for the little brooks to begin tumbling down the hillsides again, brooks created by the thaw and melt of late winter. Each starts with a single drop of water, then grows into a trickle over the rocks; eventually, the brooks gurgle and chatter, alive with their new freedom from ice. Those brooks sing one of the true songs of the season.

By now, in some years, we can see the swelling of buds on the lilacs and rhododendrons, and an amber new glow to the twigs of the weeping willows. A crocus may pop up any day now, and there is usually some stirring in the flower gardens from the daffodils and tulips.

When any of these signs show, I get impatient, carried away. I start listening for the spring peepers and wondering when the red-winged blackbirds will arrive. I drive to the ponds, searching for tree swallows, and hike into the low-lying swamps, half expecting to see the marsh marigolds in bloom.

More often than not, I'm caught looking too far ahead. The ponds

are usually still locked in ice on my first visits, the bogs still frozen. The red-wings and swallows aren't late; I'm early. They'll be here in due time. They always are. There are no flowers blooming down in the bog, but why should there be? It's not time yet; it's only February, after all.

These realizations can be deeply disappointing, particularly after several days of 50 degrees and teasing sunshine. So I seek out my old standby, the skunk cabbage. I may not be able to find a red-winged blackbird when I want it, or a marsh marigold or spring peeper, but the skunk cabbage never lets me down. It is reassurance—a promise that can be believed.

Long before spring comes, the skunk cabbage pokes through the frozen muck and ice of the bog. There are years—like this one—when the weed is up before Christmas. The spikelike sprout appears way before there should be any thoughts of spring. It stands there through all the weeks of snow and ice, all the false springs and late storms, green and healthy. Late cold snaps and storms may slow its growth, but they never kill it. It is a constant reminder that winter does not last forever, that snow and ice will eventually be gone, that greenery and new life — spring—are not that far away.

It's a unique plant, this skunk cabbage. Some people call it a wild flower, but I won't go that far. The skunk part of its name is deserved; the smell, when the plant is stepped on or crushed, is, ah, rather unpleasant. The cabbage part is from the large cabbagelike leaves on the mature plant. It is certainly not a cabbage, but rather a member of the arum genus, most of which grows in wet places.

In order to appear so early in the year, the skunk cabbage generates its own warmth. Scientists have found that a skunk cabbage thrusting up through the frost may have as much as 27 degrees more heat than the surrounding soil or air. All plants generate a certain amount of warmth, through respiration. The skunk cabbage throws off so much heat that it can grow quite easily even when the air temperature is in the low 20s. The plant literally melts its way to the surface.

Anytime now, the tightly wound spikes will open, revealing a greenish hood, which will become purplish and mottled. Inside the hood will be the plant's "blossoms," which cannot be called either pretty or fragrant. They are, in fact, so smelly that they attract more carrion flies than bees. A little later, the giant leaves will form, and for the rest of spring and all of summer the skunk cabbage will be just another green weed of the wetlands. Overlooked. Unimportant. Insignificant.

But right now the plant is important. It grows in the same places every year, and it is always up well before winter gives up for good. It reassures us that a spring will follow every winter. It is the one sign that can be counted on: the one that will be there whenever we need it.

88

The Bluebirds of Winter

It's a cold, gray morning—weather forecasters would say bitterly cold—and I'm out early. I want to see if this cold snap and the recent snowstorm have driven away the bluebirds.

Bluebirds are supposed to be migrants, warm-weather birds that spend their winters lolling in the sunshine of the deep South. But for some reason a small flock of them has been staying here. I saw them regularly through the fall and early part of the winter; now I wonder if they've had enough and moved out. Or are they sticking around for the duration?

I've never quite understood how and why some birds suddenly choose not to migrate, defying instinct and eons of habit. Are they capable of making conscious decisions like that? Does one bird, a leader, tell the others that our winters aren't that tough, so let's stick around? Is it because the living down South isn't as easy as it used to be? Are birds becoming too lazy to fly that far?

Bluebirds certainly aren't the only birds that occasionally skip a year of migration. A pair of wood ducks has lingered on my brook since October—I keep wondering if the decision to stay was the gaudy male's or the seemingly meek female's—and I saw a small flock of robins on New Year's Day. A flicker, a grackle and a fox sparrow have been around my yard this winter as well. All of them should be hundreds of miles from here.

Perhaps those of us who feed birds are partly responsible. I know the grackle and fox sparrow are spending most of their time gobbling up cracked corn that is meant for the real birds of winter, the cardinals and juncos. If we didn't make food so available to them, maybe these other birds, the once-upon-a-time migrants, wouldn't have changed their lifestyles. Maybe we're upsetting the natural scheme of things with our feeders.

But that doesn't explain the bluebirds. They never come into the yard. In fact, the flock I've been watching has remained in the rocky hillside meadow since last spring. At least two pairs nested there, although not in the houses I built for them.

I pick a trail that wanders through a section of woods. The snow is crunchy now, with the surface frozen, and the walking is doubly noisy in the woods, because of the brittle leaves underneath. But these are the only sounds. No chickadees appear. No jays. No squirrels.

If these animals are intimidated by the cold, stunned into silence, how are the bluebirds —if they're here—faring?

Fox tracks follow the trail, but they are a couple of days old. Was it too cold last night for even foxes to be out? I consider for a moment following the tracks, to see if I can find where this fox is holing up; last time I did, I found a refuge beneath a small, dense hemlock. But no, this search is for bluebirds. I head straight for the meadow.

Just as I leave the woods, a grouse explodes from the snow in a whir of wings. It flies only about 50 feet, just high enough to clear the weeds, and settles at the edge of the clearing. I walk over to see what it was feeding on, and find only a handful of wild grapes, shriveled, frozen, utterly unappetizing. Pickings are getting slim out here.

I circle a thicket of briers and climb the boulder I used when checking the bluebirds last summer and fall. Then, I'd stay only long enough for a glimpse of them—just to be sure they were still around; I never looked for their nests, because I didn't want to take the chance of disturbing them.

A crow is calling from somewhere down in the valley. Three chickadees are doing gymnastics in the brush by the woods. A mocking-bird is hunched, not moving a feather, in a bush close by, so uncharac-teristically subdued it takes me several moments to notice it.

But there is no sign of the bluebirds.

I linger until the cold starts getting to me. I still don't know if the birds are really gone, or just staying in bed today. As I trudge home I wonder some more: if they migrate, do they go down the East Coast only until they find suitable weather, or do they try to make it all the way to the Gulf, or wherever their colleagues are staying?

By the time they get there, I calculate, it is almost time to turn around again. Last year, bluebirds made their first appearance here on March 20. Hardly seems worth the effort.

89

March

It's March 1. We've survived February, and now can seriously think about spring. It's March, the month of transition, the season within a season. Muddy March. Maddening March. Marvelous, magical March.

March is so many things. Icy rains and cruel winds and tantalizing May-like sunshine. It's uneven, unpredictable, unreliable. It's robins caught in snowstorms. It's the tiny frogs called spring peepers chanting one day and then huddling beneath ice the next. It can extend the season for skiers and skaters, or start the year for golfers and gardeners. Or do both.

I've always liked a description of March that I ran across in a book by Hal Borland, the late naturalist-writer from Connecticut:

"March is a tomboy with tousled hair, a mischievous smile, mud on her shoes and a laugh in her voice. She has whims and winning ways. She's exasperating, lovable, a terror-on-wheels, too young to be reasoned with, too old to be spanked. March is February with a smile and April with a sniffle. March is a problem child with a twinkle in its eye."

It's difficult, at the beginning of March, to realize what the outdoors will be like by the month's end. Each year I try to jot down the succession of changes, the series of "firsts" that March produces, and yet each year when I check these notes, I'm a little surprised by it all.

Last year, for instance, I spent March 1 ice fishing with my sons and noticed the booming of the ice. The temperature was barely 30, but ice was already starting to yield with sharp cracks, like ricocheting rifle shots, and long, low rumbles. It was like listening to winter saying goodby.

The last day of March was Easter, a perfect day, over 70 degrees. Again, the boys were fishing, but this time they were in a rubber raft, getting sunfish and sunburns. I remember watching from the shore for a time. A hawk was circling high above, riding the rising air currents, and song sparrows were singing their little hearts out. It was full-blown spring.

I know many people dislike March, and with good reason—wind and rain and slush and mud. But because there are so many things happening, it can be an exciting time, too.

There is the day the ice "goes out" on the ponds, and the day the little brooks start trickling down the hillsides. The first green grass usually shows up along those brooks, the first pussy willows bloom beside the streams, the first lively sprigs of the marsh marigold appear in the bogs. In fact, by the end of March we'll be searching for the first violets and hepaticas and other wild flowers.

About now, the first of the migrant birds return. Red-winged blackbirds and phoebes and robins and sometimes bluebirds. Then the killdeer and kingfishers and tree swallows appear. If you're lucky, you may see and hear the first flock of geese cross high overhead on its way north. If you're even luckier, or know where to look, before the month is up you may see woodcocks doing their bizarre courtship dances.

The spring peepers are always the first cold-blooded creatures to be noticed, usually with a few tentative notes when their shallow pools are still ringed in ice. By late March, their chants will be loud and long, practically nonstop around the clock. And by then other frogs and toads, and turtles and snakes, will be awakening, too.

And as for the insects, all it takes for the first ones to appear is one warm day, perhaps 60 or 70 degrees—and we always get such teasing days in March. Then the tiny midges and gnats and new hatchlings of a hundred species show up. If we have a few such days, the honeybees and bumblebees and even some butterflies may be added to the list of firsts. Unfortunately, such days also bring the first mosquitoes.

Each arrival of a migrant bird, each sprig of greenery, each hatching of an insect means progress toward spring. For that, we can endure the maddening relapses of March, and enjoy its magical parts.

After all the snow and ice of this winter, even mud sounds good. Sort of.

90

Old Grouch

OLD GROUCH IS an absolute gentleman these days. He's courteous, considerate, downright lovable. What better sign can there be that spring is creeping up on us?

Our Old Grouch is a handsome fellow, a cardinal that somehow seems redder than other cardinals. We started calling him Old Grouch early in the winter, when his disposition was a lot darker than his feathers. He snapped at other birds wanting to use the feeder, often driving everyone else away, including the only female cardinal around the yard. If birds could growl, he would have done so.

That went on all through December and January. He would appear every morning, flying up from the cedars near the marsh. Many times the female would come along, dutifully following at a distance. He would immediately strike out at the house finches and chickadees and song sparrows, dashing at them with his beak open, eyes blazing and crest raised in anger: Out of my way, small fry. Scram!

The only birds that stood up to Old Grouch were the blue jays, which are larger and even more belligerent, though there were far fewer jays this winter than in other winters. Often weeks went by without jays showing up, and during that time Old Grouch ruled the roost. Only on rare occasions would even the female cardinal attempt to eat beside Old Grouch, and then she ran the risk of being treated like a house finch. Usually, she perched in the nearby spruce and meekly waited for him to finish stuffing himself. That didn't go over very well with my wife, watching from inside the house. "Chauvinist" was probably the kindest thing she called him.

By February, however, Old Grouch started mellowing. He still didn't want to dine beside the little birds, but he was less hostile. And he would allow the female to enter the big, boxlike feeder with him. Sometimes, they came into the yard together and left together. Once, during a snowstorm, they perched side by side in the spruce for a couple of hours, sharing the shelter in quiet harmony. I kept expecting Old Grouch to send the female out into the storm for a sandwich, or at least

a sunflower seed, but he never did. When the storm subsided, shortly before dusk, both cardinals stopped at the feeder and then flew off together, toward the cedar thicket, where they spend the night.

By mid-February, when we had those below-zero nights and sunny but frigid days, Old Grouch's heart was really thawing. He started perching high in bushes and, ignoring the icy wind, tuned up his voice. Cardinals sing for the same reasons as most birds—to define their territories and to attract mates. They have rich, clear voices, and their songs are repeated whistles that bird experts translate as *birdy, birdy, birdy*. With Old Grouch, however, I think he's saying *pretty, pretty, pretty*—though I don't think he's describing his lady love, who is almost drab-colored compared with him. No, the object of this guy's affection seems to be himself.

Lately, though, Old Grouch has really turned over a new leaf, so to speak. Spring is coming, and we all know what that does to the male of the species. Any species. Courtship time does strange things to birds, almost as strange as it does to humans. Right now, Old Grouch couldn't be more solicitous of the female, more eager to please her.

No more is he driving her away from the feeder. In fact, he's now feeding her the sunflower seeds. He picks up a seed, hops over to the female, and tenderly puts it in her beak. How sweet can you get? I'm not sure that makes up for the way he treated her back there in midwinter, but she seems to appreciate the attention now.

Old Grouch has apparently won himself a mate. But I wonder how long this Sir Galahad act will continue. Can a chauvinist really turn chivalrous that suddenly?

Chances are the cardinals will nest somewhere around the marsh and the books tell me that males often continue catering to their mates, even feeding them, right through the incubation of the eggs. I'm going to have to keep tabs on this pair; I'd love to see Old Grouch get run ragged by his mate. I'd call that justice.

91

Tumbledown Brook

IT BEGINS WITH a tiny trickle, a few drops of icy water dripping from rock to rock. Somewhere up on the hill, snow is melting. Tumbledown Brook is being reborn.

At this time of year, a thousand miniature brooks are being created. Warmer weather means water, and water runs downhill. So every slope has brooks. It's that simple.

Still, Tumbledown Brook is something special. Several years ago, this chattering, clattering brook was all but destroyed. Its channels were severed by bulldozers. Its clear water was stained a muddy, sickly brown. Each spring the same image came to mind when I'd see that water: the tortured hillside was bleeding. Poets usually describe spring brooks as happy; this one was miserable. Tumbledown Brook no longer sang on its way to the river; it just oozed sadly through the scalped subsoil.

Time, though, is indeed a great healer. When the marketable timber and stone and gravel of the slope were gone, the bulldozers moved on. It then took a while, but a natural repairing process began. The desolate lower section of the hillside, which resembled a tiered desert, began to get better.

A few pine cones that had rolled down the hill from trees higher up took root and sprouted. Other plants that can survive in thin, stony soil also appeared. A huge thicket of pokeweed, which produces juicy berries that birds find irresistible, made the spot a lively place for birds until Thanksgiving, well after other prettier and "wilder" areas had been abandoned.

Numerous scars do remain, but they, too, have been softened.

Violets bloomed last summer in the old truck lane between the pines and the river. A kingfisher tunneled into the cliff left by a bulldozer's blade and raised a family there. Bank swallows inspected the cliff last spring; though they chose another area for their colony, they might be back this year.

Now, Tumbledown Brook seems to be finding its own peace. With the young trees, patches of grass, stands of weeds and even mosses and lichens on hand to hold the soil in place, the brook has resumed following a well-defined route down the slope. Again, the brook has carved a channel, curling around some rocks, rushing headlong over others. And while I wouldn't say the brook is singing, or even babbling, it is at least noisy again, sounding of early spring and freedom from ice and a stirring of new life.

So now I return to it, climbing the slope again as I did years ago, following the brook to its origins, high in the ledges. I named it Tumbledown the first time I saw it, on a mild March day when it was running at full volume, tumbling down the hill, splashing over uncountable polished rocks in a frantic dash toward the river far below.

To me, that brook became a symbol of the season, as sure a sign of impending spring as red-winged blackbirds and high-flying geese and the first woodchuck nosing around the garden. If I needed assurance that spring was coming, I'd go out and check that brook. And when it did break free, when it began trickling and gurgling, I knew that if winter was not altogether defeated, it was at least in retreat.

The brook still has a long way to go in regaining the pristine beauty of its pre-bulldozer days. Perhaps it never will; perhaps innocence lost can never be regained. The water is getting clearer, but it continues to carry some silt and sand. Many of the huge boulders that formed its falls and chutes are gone. It will be years before hemlocks and birches again crowd around, shading the brook, adding color and vitality to the scene.

But now there is hope. If left alone, the slope will someday be covered with trees again. If left alone, the brook will run clear once more. If left alone, with time, even the broken rocks now serving as the brook's bed will become smooth.

I don't know what the chances are for anything to be left alone that long. But, right now, there is hope.

92

Deermouse Tenants

Maybe I wasn't cut out to be a landlord. I'm just not very good at evictions.

It's almost time for my new tenants to arrive, and the family that leased the house for the winter shows no signs of moving out. That puts me on the spot: I have to toss them out, or else find other suitable quarters for a couple that right now is traveling hundreds of miles to spend the spring and summer here. That won't be easy; these summer residents are rather picky about where they live.

By now, the deermice should have left the birdhouse. I didn't mind at all when they took over for the winter. It gave them a safe, cozy den for the cold months, a high and dry hideaway above the meadow. But the house was built for bluebirds, and they'll be arriving anytime now. I want the house vacant and ready for them—but I hate to just kick out the deermice.

It was in late January that I discovered that the mice had moved in. On a snowy, blustery day, I happened by the field and decided to check the house nailed to a maple at the edge of a woods. From the ground I could see that the house was occupied; bits of grass and moss were protruding from the entrance hole. And I suspected mice, because they frequently move into birdhouses; I just didn't know which kind.

As with all my bluebird houses, this one has a hinged roof—it makes spring cleaning easy—and I was most cautious in opening it. Often in the past, at the instant I've lifted these lids, the mice have bolted. A blur, a glimpse, and they were gone. I wanted a good look at these squatters.

The box was filled to the top. Scattered liberally throughout the yellowing grasses and gray-green mosses were tiny fragments of blue jay feathers. These mice had an eye for interior design: The color scheme was unusual yet harmonious; flashy, but not gaudy. The blue was a nice touch.

I gently lifted out a clump of the filling and saw a bit of movement downstairs. With a twig, I carefully brushed aside the soft blankets until I found two deermice curled up side by side.

Handsome creatures: red-brown heads and backs, white beneath, huge brown eyes. They were trembling, more from fear, I'm sure, than the cold, but they made no effort to flee. I had no desire to send them out into the snow, so I quickly replaced their insulation and closed the lid.

That was several weeks ago. I figured they would be gone by March and I could have the box cleaned out in time for the bluebirds' arrival from the South. These mice, though, seem to have staked a claim to the

place; they show no signs of leaving. I suppose they've had it too easy all winter. Besides taking over the house for their sleeping quarters, they remodeled a bird's nest in a nearby bush, turning it into their pantry by filling it with assorted berries and weed seeds. Tracks in the snow showed that they probably had another cache beneath a large rock in the stone wall at the base of the maple.

Right now, I suppose, they're planning to fill the birdhouse with the patter of little feet. Lots of little feet. See what happens when you try to be a nice guy?

This is the third year for that house, and the bluebirds haven't used it yet. The first year, some birds—I never learned what kind—built a foundation of a nest with stiff twigs, then abandoned the idea. Apparently they decided the place wasn't big enough for their needs. Last spring, a pair of tufted titmice made their home there, and as far as I know were successful in raising their family. Now it's the mice.

I have no real objections to titmice, or to chickadees, which moved into three other houses last summer. I consider myself open-minded, an equal-opportunity landlord (except when it comes to starlings; they're not welcome), but I have to admit that I prefer bluebirds.

Bluebirds are among the most desirable birds around. Not only are they spectacular to look at—there is no purer blue anywhere—and delightful to listen to, but they are exemplary neighbors, as well. They live chiefly on nasty caterpillars and ugly insects, seldom engage in domestic squabbles and stay out of my strawberry patch. What more could I ask?

Unfortunately, bluebirds are not very common these days, and one of the reasons is the absence of the hollow trees they formerly used as nesting sites. Hence the need for birdhouses.

Two years ago, a couple of bluebirds used another of my houses, but the following winter a squirrel chewed the entrance hole until it was about twice its original size, and the birds did not renew their lease last spring. A pair must have nested somewhere in the area, though, because I saw them throughout the summer. I suppose that means they really don't need my accommodations after all, but I like to think they would prefer these strategically placed, well-ventilated apartments, with exquisite views, to some stuffy room in a rotting stump.

That's why I'm putting the deermice on notice. The house they helped themselves to is the best of the bunch, the penthouse suite. It has a commanding view of a high meadow that once was a pasture. Wild roses grow up there, and there are a few old apple trees along the edge that still blossom each spring. Grasshoppers and other insect goodies are plentiful all summer.

I'm even willing to let the mice come back next winter, if they wish, but right now I'd like to see them hit the road. Bluebirds are on the way. They've had reservations for three years now; it's about time they get to use their place.

Maybe I'll give the mice one more week.

93

Waking the Toads

THIS IS THE week I usually start spading my garden. I figure the toads have slept long enough.

Each spring when I turn over the soil in my little garden, I uncover some toads that have spent the winter there. Some years I'll find only one or two; other times I'll run across half a dozen or more. They've burrowed down six or eight or ten inches and snoozed away the cold months.

I don't mind at all. I like having toads in the garden. They're more efficient at keeping down the insect population than most sprays. I remember reading somewhere that a single adult toad will consume about 10,000 insects over a three-month summer. That's a lot of bugs. They'll gobble up beetles, caterpillars, grasshoppers, moths, spiders and practically anything else that might invade a garden. Even gypsy moths. That by itself makes toads worthy neighbors.

So toads are always welcome out there. They're not the most attractive of creatures, of course, and it can still be a little bit startling to be pulling out weeds or picking peas and suddenly come face to face with one. It will be sitting there, in the shade beneath the vines and leaves, all hunched up: huge head, bulging eyes, rough and warty skin.

They're always fat—we apparently have a good supply of insects— and look very contented. Just waiting for another insect to pass by, so that they can flick out that long, sticky tongue and reel in another morsel. The speed with which they snap out their tongues is incredible—scientists assert that it takes only 15-hundredths of a second to flick the tongue, catch the insect and pop it into the mouth. That's faster than the human eye can follow, but toads do it so effortlessly, so

nonchalantly, I sometimes think they have an easier time making their living than almost any other creature I know.

The toads seem to realize they have nothing to fear from us. Even when we accidentally uncover their hiding places, they usually only blink at the unexpected sunlight and wait for us to replace their canopy. Sometimes one will take a step or two backward, toward deeper shade, but they seldom make any effort to flee. The garden is their home; we're merely caretakers.

They continue feeding in the garden until the first frosts of autumn eliminate the insects; then they start digging in for hibernation. Most years, I'll rake a big pile of maple leaves into the garden, partly because some nutrients will leach from the leaves into the soil over the winter, and partly because it's easier than bagging those leaves. The toads seem to like the leaves; often, the more leaves I deposit in the fall, the more toads I'll find in the spring. With the insulating cover of leaves above them, the toads don't have to burrow so deep to escape the frost line. They're as lazy as I am.

Knowing they may be only a few inches down, I dig rather carefully in spring. There have been a few times over the years when I decapitated a hibernating toad with my spade. That's not a pleasant feeling. I know that if I waited a little longer to begin spading, if I waited until the ground was warmer, the toads would awake on their own and be out of my way—but it's not easy to be patient at this time of year. When the frost leaves the soil and the spring peepers are calling and the red-winged blackbirds are back, something compels me to start gardening. Instincts from a farming heritage, I suppose.

Last spring, my timing was just about right, from the toads' point of view. They were just about to get up anyway. We had had a few days in the 50s, and the toads' alarm clock was ringing. I uncovered four of them—without injuring any—and all four were half awake. They were sluggish and groggy—exactly how I feel most mornings—and I expected them to stretch and yawn at any moment. Instead, they waved their front feet at me rather feebly and tried to dig back under the surface. After five months' sleep, they still wanted to roll over for five more minutes.

Once fully awake, the toads will leave the garden and head for water. April is mating season, and soon the marsh down the hill will ring with the toads' high-pitched trills. It's the only time of year when the toads seem excited about anything. They can even drown out the spring peepers' cries. They hurry through their rituals much faster than the tiny frogs, though, and in a matter of a couple of weeks the females will string their jellylike eggs along the weeds at the water's edge. Immediately after that, all the adults will return to land, heading their separate ways. Back to gorging themselves on bugs.

I have no idea whether the same toads return to my garden each spring, or, for that matter, how the babies ever find their way up the slope, over a road, through the woods, over the stone walls and into the garden. Yet each year, not only do adults appear in the yard but about two months later there are always some members of the new generation showing up. Must be some sort of homing instinct. Whatever it is, I find it rather remarkable and reassuring. Supposedly, only five per cent of the eggs survive long enough to produce toads, but with each female laying up to 12,000 eggs, we're not likely to have a shortage of insect controllers for our string beans and zucchini and tomatoes.

All of that is on my mind as I start spading the garden. I do my digging very slowly, because there is much to enjoy. I like seeing the earthworms wriggling in the turned-over soil. I like watching the robins gather around the yard, waiting for me to leave so they can attack those worms. I still relish just smelling the warming and fertile earth. But perhaps most of all, I like finding those drowsy toads and "helping" them get started on another year.

Like the countryside itself, they have been asleep long enough. It's time to get going again.

94

Promise of the Buds

At first, you have to look closely to see just a faint blush of pink. Then, one day, you notice a definite reddening as you drive by. Soon, the twigs are fairly glowing. Spring has come to the apple orchard.

There are a number of other places where seasonal changes can be read at a glance. The bog is one—skunk cabbage and marsh marigolds are among the first plants to regain their greening vitality—but exploration there often leaves you up to your knees in soft, squishy mud. The orchard is an easier place to walk, and the promise is so encouraging.

Mention the promise of apple trees, and most people think only of the big, showy blossoms you'll find in late April or May, and I'll agree there are few better times to be living in apple country. But this time— right now—is pretty good too.

I've long had a special feeling for apple orchards. Like many others, I make it a point to wander among the trees in blossom time, admiring the beauty. I also go out often to check on the ripening progress throughout the late summer. I'm there when the first picking takes place, as much for the feeling as for the taste. I go back after first frost, to breathe in the tantalizing aromas. I'll roam old, abandoned orchards in winter just to see the animal tracks in snow, to see if deer are eating the windfalls. In late winter, I check again for grouse that sometimes sneak in and munch on some of the infant buds.

And I go back when sunshine and climbing temperatures start the sap pulsing through the trees' veins, shaking the twigs and branches awake after months of dormancy. It's possible to see similar revivals in other trees and bushes, of course—the maples, the osier dogwoods, the willows—but I prefer the apples.

I'm not sure just why. Maybe it's because I know the reddening twigs mean so much more life is coming, from the blossoms to the fruit. Maybe it's because I still associate the early-spring orchard glow with the arrival of bluebirds, which once frequented orchards in the days before heavy chemical sprays. And maybe it's because few other trees seem to need this annual revival as much as apple trees.

In late winter, there are few trees as forlorn as the apples. Those already pruned—a necessary process for commercial orchards—look absolutely butchered. Branches are sawed off at awkward angles; much of the growth of the previous season lies on the ground or is heaped into piles as discarded brush. It always seems too much has been pruned away. If I were running a commercial orchard, I'd probably do the same, but as a casual visitor I often wonder if it is necessary that each tree be forced into the same, unnatural shape.

Even more grotesque, more forlorn, are the trees that were pruned for years, then abandoned. As long as they are alive, the trees will send out new shoots each year, always reaching toward the sun. These new vertical twigs clash with the symmetry of the pruned tree; orchardists want their trees reaching out, not up, for heavier production and easier picking. In winter, abandoned trees look eerie, almost otherworldly. The longer the trees are neglected, the stranger they look. Somehow, when I see trees like this in winter, I never expect them to have leaves again, never mind blossoms and apples.

But the day comes when there is that mysterious flickering of new life down in the roots and in the bark and in tips of twigs. The change is subtle at first, barely discernible. But the pulse of the sap quickens as the days grow longer, and gradually the color returns to the outer twigs. It's a bit of triumph; it means the old trees have survived another winter and just might produce one more season of blossoms, one more crop of apples. Most of that fruit will be misshapen and perhaps wormy, but right now that doesn't matter. Not at all.

Spring is returning to the orchards, those thriving and those abandoned. Not as many bluebirds will be there—not nearly enough—and it will be a while yet before leaves hide the scars of pruning, but the glow of life is back. It carries so many promises. It assures us of white and pink beauty in May, of vibrant greenery through the summer, of bountiful fruit and alluring fragrances in autumn.

It's all there now, in the simple coloring of some simple twigs. But its significance is far from simple. It's magical.

95

Dad

I'M THINKING TODAY of Dad. With spring on the horizon, he must be itching to get out in the fields. It hurts so much that he cannot.

My father, a man of the soil, considered plowing one of his favorite chores. It was like taking part in the reawakening of the land, he'd say, a way of helping the natural forces get another cycle of growth and harvest in gear. Nothing happens until you plow and plant, he'd say.

Now, Dad is confined to a wheelchair. The man who was plowing long and straight furrows behind a team of horses before World War I can only watch the coming of spring from a window. In fact, from that window, he can't even see the open fields; his view is limited to two small-town streets.

In most areas of his life, Dad was as practical and unemotional as any man I've met. He lived simply and quietly, concerned chiefly with doing what had to be done. Whether he was fixing cars—he was a mechanic during most of my growing-up years—or milking cows or husking corn or chopping weeds, he faced every task with the same attitude: It has to be done, so let's get at it.

Except for plowing. That was special.

Even in the years when he had to work off the farm, he made a point of being there for the plowing. Once I thought it was because he didn't trust my brothers and me to do the job right; our furrows were never as straight as his. But later I realized there was more to it.

Dad wouldn't say then that he did the plowing himself just because he enjoyed it. That wasn't his style. Only much later did he admit to the combination of euphoria and silent satisfaction he got from opening the soil, drinking in the earthy aroma, helping set spring in motion.

Those days seem long ago now.

He was sturdy and solid then; his calloused hands both skilled and strong. He never seemed to tire. Now, as he faces his 89th spring, and the second at the window, he is thin, frail, and virtually helpless. A stroke a year and a half ago cruelly robbed him of his vitality, leaving him partially paralyzed and without most of his speaking ability. With an earlier loss of hearing, he has great difficulty communicating. Mom usually can understand what he's trying to say, but maybe that's due more to their being together for 59 years than to her actually making out the words.

But there are some things that don't have to be said.

His days revolve around visits from sons and daughters and grandchildren, and the cards and letters from those who live far away. But much time is still spent alone at the window.

Winter must be painfully long for the aged and infirm, but in Dad's case I think spring may be more difficult to endure. Right now, there must be a hundred thoughts on what he used to do, what he would want to do.

If the buds on the maples outside his window are starting to open, he may be reminded of the fruit trees he used to prune each year. If a boy wanders by with a puppy, he might think of the calves we usually had in early spring. If somebody is digging in a flower bed up the street, I'm sure he realizes it is time for somebody to be plowing those fields—still his fields—once more.

Somebody else. Not Dad. Ever again.

That's what I'm thinking today. And it hurts.

96

Resurrection

Walk the woods now and you see them almost everywhere: the fallen trees, the reminders of Hurricane Gloria. But soon, if you look closely, you'll be able to see what happens when a tree falls in the forest. All sorts of plants rush to fill the void.

It's been nearly six months now since the hurricane ripped through southern New England, uprooting thousands of trees, breaking off thousands more. Back in the forests, away from roads, most of those victims are still lying where they fell. In most cases, the logs will remain untouched for years to come, until they eventually molder and disintegrate.

Keep in mind, however, that the toppling of a tree in the woods is not a tragedy—certainly not on a par with the loss of a cherished oak or maple or hemlock in somebody's yard. No, in the forest, when a tree goes down it simply means there now is room for new plants and another generation of trees to take hold. Even the decay of a tree adds nourishment to the soil, nourishment that will aid the replacement plants. Nothing is ended. There is a recycling, a continuity.

All winter I've been trying to remember that, trying to keep in mind the fact that all the trees lying strewn about the woods still serve a purpose. It hasn't been easy.

With spring approaching, this self-healing of the forest will become evident. In the next several weeks, tiny sprigs of green will appear beside the fallen trees. They may be wild flowers, perhaps violets or Dutchman's-breeches or anemones, plants that until now had no chance to sprout because no sunshine could reach through the tight canopy of leaves and needles. Now, with a hole poked in that canopy, countless seeds that had been patiently waiting their turn will flicker to life, send down roots and send up shoots. There is seldom a shortage of seeds around; they are blown in or carried in by birds and other animals. All they need is space and sunlight.

As the season progresses, as the soil warms, other plants will appear. Ferns or club mosses. Perhaps partridgeberry or pipsissewa or any of the hundred other inconspicuous plants that crowd a forest's floor whenever they get the chance. But their time, too, is usually limited. Some do not fare well in continued sunlight. Many are simply crowded out by larger plants that always seem to find open spaces in a woods, bushes such as blackberries or blueberries, the greenbriers or even mountain laurel. The competition is keen; it will be survival of the fittest.

And down there in the humus that litters every forest floor, tree seeds will begin stirring, too. They are much more deliberate but they win out in the end. Often cedars and birches sprout first when there is a large vacancy. They'll grow for a relatively short time, maybe 20 or 25 years—just long enough and tall enough to once more shade the ground, blotting out the sunshine that gave the violets and anemones their life. The flowers will vanish. So will some of the bushes.

All this time another tiny tree will be inching upward. It will start right away, this spring, when an acorn or a hickory nut or the winged seed of a maple—whatever species the fallen tree was—pops open. It may have lain there dormant for a couple of years, just waiting for the signal that for millions of such seeds never comes. Now it has that chance and it will begin growing, extremely slowly. By the time the birches die off, the oak or hickory or maple sapling will be strong enough to fill the void, to take its rightful place among the surrounding trees.

It is likely that, in the long run, our forests are going to be healthier for Gloria's visit. I remember making a tour of the state's woods with a couple of forestry experts shortly after the hurricane, and while they were genuinely concerned about the devastation we saw, they emphasized that there were some benefits to the storm. The vast majority of the trees knocked down were either diseased or weakened by poor root structures; not many solid, healthy trees went down. Remember, I'm talking about the forests here, not the lawns. People who lost favorite shade trees aren't going to believe this, but in the deep woods, the hurricane actually did some good.

What Gloria did was remove the weak, leaving more room for the strong. It's called natural thinning, and in places like pine groves, where the trees often grow too close together, it can be a blessing. With a few trees taken out, the others can spread out a bit more, dig their roots in a little deeper, extend their branches a little wider, grow a little taller — ultimately become much more valuable trees.

I tried to keep that in mind all winter as I wandered through the woods, climbing over fallen trees that blocked the trails, gazing at large stumps snapped off 20 feet above the ground. Some good will come of this, I kept telling myself. But it was not easy to accept.

Now the time is close when the wounds will start healing. When that first violet appears beside the log, when the first acorn cracks open and sends a tiny root down and a spindly sprout up, I'll feel a little better about what happened last September. I'm not sure I've ever looked forward to a spring more.

Dates of appearance
in the Providence Journal

1	April 7, 1985	33	Aug. 11, 1985	65	Dec. 27, 1987
2	April 10, 1988	34	Aug. 16, 1987	66.	Dec. 6, 1987
3	April 3, 1988	35	Aug. 18, 1985	67	Dec. 1, 1985
4	April 17, 1988	36	Aug. 3, 1986	68	Dec. 22, 1985
5	April 13, 1986	37	Aug. 10, 1986	69	Dec. 13, 1987
6	April 14, 1985	38	Aug. 17, 1986	70	Dec. 28, 1986
7	April 26, 1987	39	Aug. 31, 1986	71	Dec. 29, 1985
8	April 12, 1987	40	Aug. 25, 1985	72	Dec. 21, 1986
9	May 5, 1985	41	Sept. 1, 1985	73	Jan. 5, 1986
10	May 15, 1988	42	Sept. 20, 1987	74	Jan. 9, 1986
11	May 22, 1988	43	Sept. 7, 1986	75	Jan. 13, 1985
12	May 11, 1986	44	Sept. 14, 1986	76	Jan. 4, 1987
13	May 3, 1987	45	Sept. 6, 1987	77	Jan. 18, 1987
14	May 26, 1985	46	Sept. 27, 1987	78	Jan. 3, 1988
15	May 24, 1987	47	Sept. 29, 1985	79	Jan. 25, 1987
16	May 31, 1987	48	Sept. 28, 1986	80	Jan. 31, 1988
17	June 17, 1984	49	Oct. 21, 1984	81	Feb. 1, 1987
18	June 5, 1988	50	Oct. 28, 1984	82	Feb. 10, 1985
19	June 15, 1986	51	Oct. 6, 1985	83	Feb. 8, 1987
20	June 14, 1987	52	Oct. 4, 1987	84	Feb. 14, 1988
21	June 1, 1986	53	Oct. 25, 1987	85	Feb. 15, 1987
22	July 6, 1986	54	Oct. 20, 1985	86	Feb. 16, 1986
23	June 30, 1985	55	Oct. 26, 1986	87	Feb. 23, 1986
24	June 28, 1987	56	Oct. 19, 1986	88	Feb. 21, 1988
25	July 5, 1987	57	Nov. 1, 1987	89.	Mar. 1, 1987
26	July 15, 1984	58	Nov. 3, 1985	90	Mar. 22, 1987
27	July 14, 1985	59	Nov. 17, 1985	91	Mar. 6, 1988
28	July 29, 1984	60	Nov. 11, 1984	92	Mar. 9, 1986
29	July 27, 1986	61	Nov. 8, 1987	93	Mar. 30, 1986
30	July 24, 1988	62	Nov. 23, 1986	94	Mar. 31, 1985
31	July 20, 1986	63	Nov. 22, 1987	95	Mar. 27, 1988
32	July 7, 1985	64	Nov. 29, 1987	96	Mar. 16, 1986